COMIC
PERSUASION

COMIC PERSUASION

MORAL STRUCTURE IN BRITISH COMEDY FROM SHAKESPEARE TO STOPPARD

ALICE RAYNER

University of California Press
Berkeley · Los Angeles · London

University of California Press
Berkeley and Los Angeles, California

University of California Press, Ltd.
London, England

©1987 by
The Regents of the University of California

Library of Congress Cataloging-in-Publication Data
Rayner, Alice.
  Comic Persuasion.
  Includes index.
    1. English drama (Comedy)—History and criticism.
2. Literature and morals—Great Britain. 3. Utopias in
literature—Great Britain. I. Title.
PR631.R39 1987   822'.0523'09353   86-28281
ISBN 0-520-05917-4 (alk. paper)

Printed in the United States of America

1 2 3 4 5 6 7 8 9

To Eric

Contents

Acknowledgments

This book owes its existence to the counsel of Bert O. States of the University of California, Santa Barbara, who insisted from the beginning that the idea of "use and delight" was worth investigating and gave freely of his time and insight to the development of the manuscript. I am deeply indebted to the generous encouragement and advice of Professor States. I would also like to thank Professor Mark Rose for his helpful comments on an early draft. For encouragement and an eye for clarity throughout, I thank John Harrop.

Introduction

I began this inquiry looking for characteristic ways that comedy uses and shapes moral material. My premise was that comedy is a special instance of the tension between use and delight because of its peculiar habit of laying claim to moral material and simultaneously denying any claim to seriousness. If as a rule comedy is the most delightful of the genres, it is also the most subversive. Our delight in wicked characters and antisocial behavior is only the most obvious example of the ways in which the aesthetic, experiential, or "indulgent" pleasure challenges the formal and ethical pleasure in which virtue is rewarded and vice is punished. On the other hand, in taking material from a social and ethical context, comedy consistently proclaims its usefulness: in satire it attacks social rigidity, institutional hypocrisy, human absurdity; in romance it celebrates the possibilities for unity, integration, and continuation of the world: the genre has the capacity to offer hope as well as correction.

My invocation of Horace's ancient formula *utile et dulce* is no more than a starting point; it provides a convenient summation of a complex interaction between pleasure and moral import. I make every effort to avoid the idea that delightful or aesthetic elements are the sweet coating for the bitter pill of moral usefulness or, in other words, that form is a vehicle for content. The formula is not a theorem that requires application to the "problem" of comic plays. We need not assume that Horace is an authority or that his formula is a rule to appreciate *ars poetica* as a complex negotiation between the worlds of artifice and reality. Comedy emphasizes that negotiation because it speaks equally to its own artifice and its audience. "Use and delight" indicates a range of capacities that create moral tension in the process of giving pleasure to an audience; it need not indicate categories for formal devices, some of which are delightful, others instructive.

In pursuing the investigation, then, I kept Horace in the background and began not with theory but with plays that have in common only that they are reasonably familiar, reasonably comic, and all British. The choice of British comedy was largely pragmatic: comic subtleties, I believe, are clearest in one's native language. But by keeping the study culture bound, I also meant to reinforce the idea that comedy is bound to its immediate social and linguistic context; its moral material is embedded in specific social and linguistic assumptions. For whatever universal principles there may be in the *comic*, rhetorical habits and changing social values inform our understanding of both humor and moral import. As a genre, comedy responds to its immediate milieu more readily than other dramatic and literary forms. Indeed, that responsiveness is one of its characteristics: the persuasiveness of comic rhetoric relies heavily on a context shared by artifice and audience.

This book is not a historical survey of British comedy, in spite of the historical order of the discussion. Such a continuity is not as crucial as the pattern of relations. In approaching the plays before theories, I derive a mapping of comic habits that I call rhetorical rather than generic or historical. The "map" in the first chapter is a scheme that indicates rhetorical directions or polarities within which a comedy will persuade its audience to accept a system of values that are equally moral and aesthetic. Values may be critical or celebratory; they may imply or deny actuality; we can see differences most clearly, however, in the comparisons with other comedies. To locate Shaw in an area where *use* and *dystopia* overlap, for example, makes an assertion about the nature of Shaw's comedies; but the location also places Shaw in relation to the *use* of Steele's sentimentality and to Jonson's *dystopia*, a relation that is not as intuitively obvious as the relation of Shaw and Stoppard in their habit of paradox.

The rhetorical map avoids the form-and-content dichotomy. One might say, for example, that all comedies in some way are "about" desire and restriction or about human biological appetites in the process of social integration. But those topics are more than subject matter. In comedy, appetite and desire are elements of aesthetic pleasure: comic subversiveness and comic delight come out of a resistance to "topics" and an insistence on the immediate gratification of performance. As I note in the first chapter, comedy occurred in performance before it gained generic distinction. Village maskers or mummers or clowns intentionally disrupt social coherence with their antics; revelry breaks the boundaries, restrictions, and forms of order, and the impulses for disruption inform the dramatic genre we call comedy. Mockery and ritual license carry over into the discourse of comedy, making an uncomfortable and disconcerting alliance with dramatic form and its capacity to suggest moral precepts.

In its structural habits comedy leads toward unity and wholeness. But because the comic impulse is never-ending, it requires an artificial closure. The marriage that customarily ends a comedy discloses an implicit ideal of order and integration that in its own way subverts the never-ending playfulness of comic disruption. The rhetoric of comedy employs contradictory kinds of desire: for disruption and integration, indulgence and harmony, revelry and virtue, correction and celebration. The comic artifact can represent, signify, and reflect a reality, but it can also deny any reality other than itself. The comic recipe is enormously variable: as it weighs its proportions of usefulness and delight it demonstrates its own desire to be in the world and exempt from worldly demands, to be free as well as efficacious, or, perhaps, to be efficacious because it is free. The comic, however, is never free of its practitioners. In the following chapters I discuss the strategies of some of those practitioners.

1

Moral Fiction and Comic Delight

Comedy has had no history, because it was not at first
treated seriously.

Aristotle, *Poetics*

Comedy is still a difficult genre to treat seriously. Since Aristotle, however, it has accumulated both a history and plenty
of notice.[1] Although it is the genre of playfulness, ludicrous
and deliberately unserious, involving situations and characters that are "without pain," it nonetheless has aroused moral
concern throughout its history. For all its playfulness it en-
gages moral and ethical material, which it appears either to
trivialize or to mock. It customarily abuses whatever is most
sacred or serious in the social sphere (marriage, church, state,
ethical dilemma), isolates that material from the sphere of
consequence and delights in its own irreverence. Yet at the
same time comedy consistently appears to have a didactic
purpose, suggesting an ethically better world.

In the *Poetics* Aristotle makes a sketchy attempt to give
comedy a history, that is to say, an origin. But as he notes,
there were already "certain defining characteristics" in com-

1. Two translators give different readings of the passage at 1449b of Aristotle's *Poetics*. The first, S. H. Bucher, quoted in the epigraph of this chapter
(*The Poetics of Aristotle* [London: Macmillan, 1907]), offers a felicitous render-
ing: "Comedy has had no history." The second is more recent and more literal: "Comedy did escape notice in the beginning" (Gerald Else, *Aristotle: Poetics* [Ann Arbor: University of Michigan Press, 1967]). Bucher's translation,
very much of the nineteenth century, implies ideas of origin and progress,
Else's, ideas of attention. The translations may seem less contradictory, however, if we say that attention itself creates a history. My own study simply
"gives notice" to comedy, but it is salutary to remember that notions of comedy are embedded in time and that understanding is historical.

edy before it took its historical place in the dramatic contests: before, that is, the Athenian poet Crates followed the Sicilian example and added plot; before the lampooning mode was compressed into the parabasis of Old Comedy; and before the comic poets were granted their official choruses for the contests. Aristotle does not define the predramatic characteristics for us, but he does imply a principle of comedy in these murky origins. He reminds us that comedy was a performance before it was a dramatic genre. Such performance, moreover, consists of an immediate interaction between "audience" and "performers" in a relationship of allowed abuse. The lampooning mode is a form of verbal attack, analogous to the mock attack in certain rituals, but also related to the mock aggression that the likes of Freud or Koestler have identified in the structure of jokes. The lampoon is doubly "unhistorical," doubly unworthy of serious consideration, because its efficacy, dependent on the immediate context of its audience, is utterly transient and because its very intent, to ridicule and parody all forms of seriousness and authority, is potentially dangerous. The principle of predramatic comedy is a principle of aggression in transit. The lampoon, like our own celebrity "roasts," requires an immediate context and awareness shared by audience and performers, and neither, perhaps, is really worthy of serious historical consideration. The ethical concern for plot and character do not belong to the predramatic mode: they are added when comedy is grafted to tragic form. The social and psychological satisfactions that arise from the safe abuse of authority are not necessarily commensurate with the ethical satisfactions that plot and character provide. When we try to reconcile moral value and comic impulses, we often find that these two varieties of satisfaction collide. It may be helpful to remember, then, that comedy is historically a grafted form, combining the delights of invective that rely on an immediate context and interaction with an audience and plot and character that lead toward ethical consideration of an action.

The unity of usefulness and delight that Horace recommends becomes a moral tension in comedy because the genre converts the materials of the social world to its own delightful ends. In comedy the playwright implicates society in a literary and theatrical art form; thus the comedy itself must answer two questions: is it useful and, if so, in what manner? Because comedies, especially satiric comedies, are bound by time and social convention, relying on a contemporaneous situation for their humor, they function more explicitly as social documents than do tragedies. It is especially difficult to force a comedy into the mold of precept and example or to reduce its characters, plot, and moral to a proposition. Tragedy presents less difficulty insofar as character and action take idealized form. Comedy customarily uses disruptive techniques to subvert the ideal. The very notion of precept and example derives from plot and character and the ethical sphere of tragedy. When scholars apply the tragic model to comedy, they derive the ethical formula that comedy rewards virtue and punishes vice. But this formula circumvents the dangerous aspects of comedy.

The "danger" of comedy lies in the immediacy of its concerns, in the actuality of the objects of derision. Comedy strikes too close to home, threatens the authority of real social or moral institutions, and all too readily shows life as it is rather than as it ought to be. Critics of comedy have always warned against deriding those members of society who deserve respect. Cicero commended the death penalty for anyone who composed a song that "contained a slander or insult to anyone else." "This was an excellent rule; for our mode of life ought to be liable to judgment by the magistrates and the courts of law, but not by clever poets."[2] The extremity of the penalty speaks emphatically of the fear of comedy's power and of the presumption that the invective of comedy indeed functions as a kind of public trial. Cicero complains that the object of the satire or slander is helpless to defend himself, for the satiric poet ridicules in public but the license of his fictive forms protects him.

---

2. Cicero, *De republica / De legibus*, trans. Clinton Walker Keyes (Cambridge, Mass.: Harvard University Press, 1928), 4.10.11.

Comedy is grounded on the social plane but with its devices of delight seeks to sever any connection to social consequence. Even as it claims the exemption of fiction, however, it acknowledges the integration of the real and the fictive. It enlists the audience to its moral realm. A fundamental convention in comedy is the frank acknowledgment of the audience and the open complicity between the imaginary world and the real one. Through direct address or an aside to the audience, a comic character can move freely in both fiction and reality and unite the real and the fictional in a single ethical space. Such a character bridges the ontological gap between fiction and reality. Moreover, comedy insists on being efficacious. In the most immediate and obvious way, laughter is evidence of effectiveness; in a more attenuated way, pleasure is evidence of a moral satisfaction. Laughter and pleasure prove that the audience is engaged with both method and matter.

Comedy is thus the genre most vulnerable to moral attack, the one that has had the greatest historical difficulty finding theoretical or moral justification. If it is not a serious genre, it may not be worth serious scrutiny; if it is serious, it may threaten the moral fabric of society. The genre represents an indulgence that is either trivial or actively harmful. Although the anticomic argument is blind to the chasm between reality and a fictional representation, comedy itself asks to have it both ways, to be inside *and* outside the ethical sphere of its audience. If vice, forbidden indulgences, lust, or infidelity were not ethically charged in the real world, they would have little interest in the comic world, and comedy would lose a large portion of its subject matter. On the other hand, what is comic is not so much the subject matter as an attitude, and comedy appears to teach a dangerous attitude.

An oddity of comic theory is that although we can easily identify a comedy, we find the comic essence difficult to isolate. We separate the psychology of laughter from the structures of comedy, but the presence of either laughter or a certain structure seems to identify comedy. Tragedy presents the opposite problem. We have a strong sense of the tragic essence but slightly less capacity to identify what is truly a tragedy. The problem is at least as old as Aristotle. The tragic is both more of an essence and more elusive than the comic: relatively few particular instances qualify as tragic unless that category is used loosely to define any pathetic situation or story ending in death. Comedy, conversely, sprawls out into individual instances. It has many conventions and habits but seems to have no essential quality and no "history" that allows us to take it seriously. It seems to have begun in performance, as spontaneous mockery of social coherence.

Tragedy is hardly ever attacked on the basis of its moral usefulness because it is inherently a moral genre. It functions according to an operative order; adheres closely to metaphysical, if not religious, dimensions of experience; and often serves to prove the effectiveness of a universal justice. Perhaps it would be more accurate to say that tragedy assumes an absolute order and an effective machinery of justice that operate in both cosmological and social realms. The form itself, in other words, tends to confirm whatever social and judicial system exists outside the tragic fiction. In this sense, tragedy is a conservative genre, a ready-made vehicle for cultural values. Morality is fundamental in its structure. The particulars of a historical situation lend themselves to universal principles. The tragic structure enhances whatever values function in the contemporaneous situation—whether honor or duty or reason.

Comedy insists on being understood in the concrete and particular. We do not often claim, for example, that a comedy by Jonson is more or less of a comedy than one by Shakespeare. We may say one comedy is more or less funny, more or less realistic. We are inclined, however, to say that because Jonson gives us a tragic experience different from the one that Shakespeare gives, Jonson's tragedies are not real tragedies— as though there could be genuine tragedy and false tragedy. Comedy satisfies an immediate appetite and an appetite for the immediate. Tragedy seems to have centrifugal and centripetal forces because it encloses experience even as it leads out to infinite dimensions. Comedy, as a social rather than an individual genre, grounds social forms in a collective, immediate experience. Tragedy seems thus to be the genre of the internal and eternal, comedy of the external, social, and temporary. If tragedies let us glimpse the infinite, comedies close in upon the finite.

This is not to say that tragedies have no social, ethical, and temporal foundation or that comedies afford none of the satisfactions of a universal principle. From the broad perspective of myth, we can say with Susanne Langer that comedy celebrates the pure sense of life and that it springs from a fundamental rhythm in life itself or with Northrop Frye that the persistence of comic structure is analogous to the ritual return of spring.[3] The comic form repeats the irrepressible force of life over death; the comic marriage symbolically duplicates the mystery of renewal, offering the hope that finite existence is nonetheless perpetual and that the world as we know it can begin again, renewed and refreshed. But that renewal arrives in the material cloak of the temporal, social, and therefore ethical world. Comedy implies that a better, happier world is possible, albeit improbable; tragedy leaves the world behind, its ethical structure cleansed but otherwise unchanged. The citizens of Thebes get rid of the plague, certainly, and by implication can get on with their lives, but that cleansing is almost irrelevant by contrast to our concern for Oedipus. Imagine the difference if Oedipus were somehow able to find the right girl to marry. Such an event would shift our attention to the public display of renewal and revitalization with the added ethical dimension of happiness.

For all its mythic significance, a marriage is also a social contract. Without denying a deep connection to a seasonal or

---

3. Susanne K. Langer, "The Great Dramatic Forms: The Comic Rhythm," in *Feeling and Form* (New York: Charles Scribner's Sons, 1953), pp. 326–50; Northrop Frye, "Archetypal Criticism: Theory of Myths," in *Anatomy of Criticism* (Princeton, N.J.: Princeton University Press, 1957), pp. 131–239. The debt to Frye in the fearful symmetry of my diagram will be obvious. My scheme is not as comprehensive as Frye's, nor is it meant to suggest an archetype of comedy. I hope, however, that like Frye's *Anatomy*, it suggests dynamic principles, not proscriptive categories, and will likewise be used not to distort particular forms into abstractions but to illuminate consistencies and differences.

biological pattern, the ending of comedy in a marriage presents happiness or a desirable condition on the level of social experience. Moreover, the context of that social experience is time, change, and relative ethical values rather than transcendence and the absolute. Renewal is an ongoing process in and of the world, and by whatever magic renewal is possible (where would Oedipus find the right girl?), the mode of comedy is that of continuation in the world. A comic action is fulfilled in the ethical sphere as well as in a cyclic pattern, and unlike tragic fulfillment, comic fulfillment is most often located in a specific event like a marriage or the sudden arrival of the Law. Tragedy, conversely, leads toward a "nonevent"— toward a purely personal moment that is unseen and unheard, toward the compression of experience into silence, not celebration. The tragic hero is part of a social and ethical structure, to be sure, but the development of the tragic plot takes him away from both society and time into some essential moment that cannot be localized by an event unless, perhaps, that event is death. If death is not always or necessarily tragic, it is at least asocial in the extreme.

Comedy presents us with a socialized ethic rather than an individualized metaphysic. It is event oriented, so to speak. Thus in discussing comedy we are often trapped into choosing the humor or the structure of the event, its wit or its intent, its decorum or its truth, its psychological satisfaction or its social purpose. Historically, at least, the difficulty reflects the hybrid nature of comedy that grafts plot and character to the impulse for witty invective. I would like to examine what seem to me paradigmatic attempts to find forms for the contradictory elements in comedy—forms that use the tensions between pleasure, delight, ethics, and moral structure. In what ways, in other words, have comic playwrights combined the tensions of use and delight, of moral order and playful chaos, of celebration and abuse, of literary persistence and performatory transience, and the contradictory values attached to each? In what ways do comic forms appear to rise out of the intents to teach and to please? How does form rise out of the material of impermanence that is the mortal, biolog-

Rhetorical Territory of Comedy

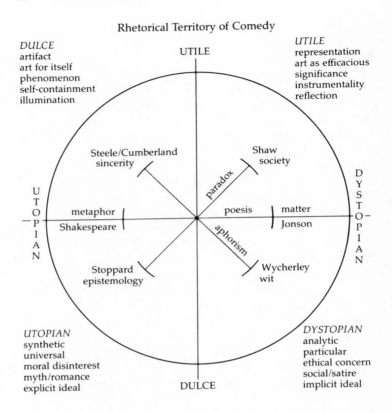

ical, appetitive, and otherwise faulty reality of human experience? More accurately, perhaps, we can ask not for the form but for the strategy that combines use and delight.

The diagram of the rhetorical territory of comedy is a hypothesis. It represents a possible order for relations between kinds of comedy and a possible range for the ethical territory of comedy. It imagines a structure for the attitudes and intentions that might contribute to the usefulness of comic forms and seeks to account for the combination of moral and aesthetic elements in expressions of comic artifice. It is meant to be a dynamic scheme, not a categorical one, allowing for changing proportions of ethical intentions and comic devices and suggesting that devices of delight are as useful as ethical intents are delightful.

The diagram maps dichotomies. I suggest broadly that comedy can either affirm and celebrate or diagnose and criticize. Intentionally, it can aim either at specific social utility or at pure delight. Any number of dichotomous terms might serve, but I have chosen *utopia* and *dystopia* to define the areas of ethical attitudes and *"utile"* and *"dulce"* (from Horace) to define the areas of intents.[4]

The placement of Shakespeare and Jonson directly on the utopian-dystopian axis may be slightly misleading, for that axis simply divides areas. The two playwrights are there primarily because the axis, for the sake of symmetry, is halfway between *utile* and *dulce*, but also because the playwrights themselves are paradigms of utopian and dystopian visions. There is no such pair on the *utile-dulce* axis both because none of the examples is equally balanced between utopian and dystopian visions and because no play discussed is either aimed so purely at *utile* that it eliminates aesthetic elements or so wholly aesthetic that it eliminates all sense of usefulness. In relation to pure *utile* and *dulce* all pairs are eccentric; Jonson and Shakespeare, however, seem to be the most perfectly balanced between the two intents.

The utopian vision affirms and celebrates the imaginary and desirable, lending itself to myth and romance because it is not bound by verisimilitude. This vision is synthetic and inclusive and not necessarily concerned with specific moral or social errors. It seems to presume an intact moral fabric. A

---

4. Albert Cook similarly uses dichotomy as an analytic principle in *The Dark Voyage and the Golden Mean: A Philosophy of Comedy* (New York: Norton, 1966). In Cook's scheme, the probable includes the world as it is and as it can be known rationally and predicted generally; the wonderful includes the desirable conditions of life sought through the imagination. Cook's probable might include certain aspects of what I call dystopian and utilitarian, and the wonderful might include the utopian and *dulce* elements of comedy, though for Cook the wonderful is not really a part of the comic world but distinguishes idealism, artist, symbol, and individual (which belong more to tragedy) from the rational, social, and conceptual (which are comedy's method for "attacking human experience").

more unified vision of a whole than the dystopian vision, the utopian vision is synthetic rather than diagnostic. It seems less interested in argumentation and specific ethical questions than in the integration of disparate or paradoxical parts. It mystifies experience instead of critically diagnosing it. In the utopian vision, moral structure is a matrix against which most actions and characters can be accepted, embraced, and incorporated on their own terms, for its attitude is affirmative and often celebratory. This vision is deeply satisfying in the same way that myths are satisfying. That is, as long as we do not ask what injustice or ethical evils the utopian vision blinds us to and as long as we do not measure it against our sense of the actual, it seems to satisfy our hopes for what ought to be.

At the opposite extreme, the dystopian vision is analytic and diagnostic. Its worldly wisdom, irony, satire, and criticism disrupt the smooth surface of actuality. It demands that we see the world as it is, which is often the same as seeing what is wrong with it. The action within a dystopian vision is more particular, more acute, and more partial than that in the utopian, a chronic agitation against the world as it is. The dystopian critique aims at intelligibility. Thus it breaks ethical questions into a manifest dialectic and polarizes moral issues. It drives toward the corrective or possibly the fatalistic rather than the cathartic, and it often raises questions of justice and punishment. On the other hand, in the dystopian vision the ideal is hidden. Although the perception of errors and failures implies an ethical standard of measurement, in a dystopian vision, that standard is generally concealed or at least not stated explicitly. The playwright may so successfully conceal his ideal that we may not know whether he is advocating or condemning the dystopian society he presents, as in the case of most Restoration comedy. The dystopia may be the least like a world we would want to live in, but often the playwright's aesthetic audacity injects positive value and acceptability. In general, however, the dystopian play presents a version of the actual as opposed to the desirable.

The dystopian vision employs more humored or typed characters than the utopian. This is not to say that the utopian vision cannot use such characters but that they are better suited to the structure of argumentation. They tend to be univocal and represent a generality more than a particularity. The conventional example of such characters comes from Ben Jonson's comedies of humor, but similar examples come from Bernard Shaw and the Restoration comedies. One common complaint against all these playwrights is that their characters are one-dimensional. The objection suggests that the characters are not as fully human as those of, say, Shakespeare. Shaw's characters, less obsessive than Jonson's, still seem to talk too much and feel too little, or else they seem to feel only their ideas. But these comedies have in common their use of characters to map out an ethical territory. Characters function as points on the moral plot of the dystopian landscape: they stand in a configuration of the ethical errors that the playwright sees. The *world* or society of the dystopia, by contrast, often appears to be more dimensional than the characters. Although we cannot, for example, easily take a Restoration comedy out of the Restoration, or Shaw out of the nineteenth and early twentieth centuries, or Jonson out of the bustle of the streets and fairs of seventeenth-century England, we can place a Shakespeare comedy in various historical periods and imaginative locales.

The vertical axis of *utile* and *dulce* measures the intentionality of a play. Naturally, that intentionality is deeply connected to the attitudes of utopias and dystopias, but a temporary disconnection allows us to see that an attitude is not identical to an intent. I wish to distinguish between *utile* and the usefulness of a comedy. *Utile* comprises the entire range of ethical attitudes and aesthetic delights that contribute to the usefulness of a work. As a special term it has to do with a work's instrumentality in the world—its use as an example for moral precepts rather than as an occasion for delight. A comedy on the extreme verge of *utile* would not only represent a world but would suggest that the real world could profit by following the example the comedy sets, that life would do well to imitate art. A medieval morality play or an agitprop skit might be the best examples of the extreme case. But both the sentimental comedies of the eighteenth century and the paradoxical comedies of Shaw similarly suggest that their art sends an exemplary message, although Shaw and the sentimentalists hardly send the same message.

It is impossible to separate the elements of *dulce* from those of *utile*: hence this axis does not demarcate a division. *Dulce* cannot be fully separated from ethical structure, for even the aesthetic pleasure we get from an object in itself depends on a system of qualities and preferences that conceals an ethical, if not a rational or a logical, system. But at its extreme *dulce* does not pretend to set an example. It rather presents itself as the formal, visible, or auditory arrangement of materials. It strains against ethical instrumentality to create an autonomous object, one that delights in its materiality, its pure form, its virtuosity and skill. Although *dulce* is as much a part of usefulness as *utile*, *dulce* is always in tension with the instrumental nature of a work that means to set an example. All comedies are thus conceived in usefulness, but it is still possible to put them on a scale between *utile* and *dulce* and to define their tensions in these terms. We could also call this scale the range between efficacy and art, instrument and artifice, significative and phenomenal.

Within the territories of *utile-dulce* and utopia-dystopia, the diagram also draws axes of what I call rhetorical force. The rhetoric of comedy is connected here not only to the sense of style but also to the trinity of rhetorical functions formed by literary style, ideational content, and implied authorial intent. The axes are meant to suggest that the force exerted is that complex combination of form, content, and persuasion that an audience receives. Rhetorical force, that is, functions as the communicative line between work and audience and includes the combined sense of how communication is made, what is communicated, and what implicit purpose the communication serves.[5] The implications of a rhetoric of comedy have led

5. For a study of this trinity in classical theory, see Wesley Trimpi, *Muses of One Mind: The Literary Analysis of Experience and Its Continuity* (Princeton, N.J.: Princeton University Press, 1983). I first heard Professor Trimpi discuss the *an sit*, *quid sit*, and *quale sit* of literary discourse at a lecture at Dominican College in the 1970s, and the notions stayed with me. As he explains in his

me to confine my paradigms to one language. Despite whatever universal appeal a comedy may have, it invariably creates a specific world out of a particular linguistic system. Although American, French, Italian, Greek, or Russian comedies also find ways to combine use and delight and also tend toward a synthetic or an analytic vision, they specify their comic worlds with distinctive rhetorical force. A mere tone, an inflection, a regional innuendo can make all the difference between satire or sentiment, passion or persuasion.

One can keep in hand the varied strategies for combining elements of use and delight with a utopian or dystopian perspective by confining the rhetorical paradigms to one language and one culture. My focus on British comedy is not as much for the sake of historical continuity (we might say that Jonson's world is as foreign to us as Goldoni's) as for simplicity. The lines of the rhetorical axes mark difference and opposition. In the single culture that the diagram maps, in other words, we can significantly distinguish the paradox of Shaw and Stoppard from the *poesis* of Shakespeare and Jonson and at the same time can see the opposition of Jonson and Shakespeare, Stoppard and Shaw, Wycherley and Steele. My purpose is to compare significantly different strategies in a single rhetorical tradition, though I am leaving that tradition or history as an implicit connection.

The rhetoric of the comic artifice is a matter not only of words but of a complex combination of perception, speech, character, and world in a given play. Character, for example,

---

preface (pp. xi–xii), his book examines the complexities and implications of a balance in literature between the "cognitive, the judicative and the formal" intentions, analogous to the disciplines of philosophy, rhetoric, and mathematics as well as to the Platonic distinctions of the true, the good, and the beautiful: "The right balance resembles decorum, the 'mean' and equity insofar as they, too, are all expressions of continuous qualification rather than the application of fixed criteria of literary 'rules,' moral sanctions and legal statutes. When a literary theory fails to recognize and resist any tendencies toward imbalance, it will gradually reduce literature to its cognitive 'philosophical' intention, or to its exhortatory 'rhetorical' intention, or to its purely formal 'mathematical' intention." Very roughly, my designation of utopia and dystopia would be analogous to cognitive intent, *utile* and *dulce* to formal intent, and the rhetorical axes to persuasive.

is an aspect of a play's rhetoric in the sense that dramatic character and language are coextensive. In drama, language is both the style and substance of character, giving birth to characters and supplying their "genetic code," so to speak; it is this code that generates character qualities and defines a range of possible actions. In this sense, character supplies an important part of the communicative link between play and audience. If only in a naive sense, an audience's judgment of a play is commonly based on its judgment of the characters in the play, and the perception that forms the judgment is partially based on the specific cultural context of the shared language. Such a context is gestural as much as verbal. A British shrug, for example, differs from a French or Italian shrug in rhythm, weight, and therefore meaning. Gestural language is embedded in verbal codes, and the persuasiveness of a comic rhetoric therefore depends on an audience's ability to interpret gestural significations as well as verbal statements. Gesture as much as vocabulary is crucial to comic rhetoric and to an understanding of a character's ethos. I do not mean to underestimate the broad appeal of comedies or ignore the cross-cultural comic principles. Certainly we can translate Aristophanes or Molière and retain their humor, but the texture of character perceived instinctively in a native language is partially lost in translations. At the very least, there is in performance a disjunction between a character and the translated language it speaks, as though the verbal translation did not match the gestural intention of the action. The gestalt that blends character and language with history and intention, attitude and irony, speech and gesture can be caught in a word or phrase; but that gestalt usually belongs to a native understanding.

Rhetoric creates what we often call the world of the play, a world that must be made specific and concrete for the stage. The rhetorical "worlds" designated on the axes, however, are more comprehensive than the worlds of the plays.

Poesis, for example, suggests how language itself in Jonson and Shakespeare is a site for the drama, how it has the objectivity of a locale, how it is a thing in itself. *Poesis* is not strictly bound to the actors who speak as characters, for the dialogue of the poetic play is not simply overheard conversation that happens to be in meter. It is, rather, the language of formed perceptions; containing consciousness of moral perspective, motivation, and attitude, the language itself has a character. Language is a moral and aesthetic nexus for human behavior or, to put it another way, of human behavior recast on the site of formal poetic devices. Words do not simply imitate other words. *Poesis* embodies moral attitudes, thoughts, and motivations as much as an actor embodies a character. *Poesis* is a common ground, like a theater, where playwright, character, and audience all meet; it functions as a site of action. The chronic tension between literary critics and theatrical practitioners, extreme in Renaissance drama because that drama is so "literary," might be traced to *poesis*, in which language embodies the elements of theatricality but is not wholly dependent on a physical theater. The literary critic can thus insist that he gets as much, if not more, theatricality from reading Shakespeare or Jonson as from seeing a production on the stage. The practitioner can insist that the theatricality of the language is alive only on the stage, where it can be made concrete in the actor. Both perspectives are valid if we consider language, or *poesis*, as the site of action.

By *poesis* Jonson and Shakespeare achieve the balance of *utile* and *dulce*. By contrast, paradox and aphorism are eccentric styles that overbalance in the direction of intent, whether that intent is toward *utile* or *dulce*. Those rhetorical styles speak of different cultural projections of the work into the world. Both Jonson and Shakespeare are able to use the devices of aphoristic assertiveness and paradoxical inversion because these devices can be subsumed under the larger rhetorical umbrella of *poesis*.

The specific stylistic differences between Jonson and Shakespeare are numerous. Jonson's poetic method is material and ethical whereas Shakespeare's is metaphoric and moral. Jonsonian images are inevitably concrete, physically opulent, and ethically specific. Speeches build, with each phrase a discreet entity, one brick piled up on the next, seriatim, as in Volpone's greeting prayer to his gold. As so many have complained, Jonson lets his learning show. His rhetorical display tends to be as clear as his characters' names: little is left to speculation. We see ideas grow in Shakespeare, however, and thus we believe his characters grow. In Jonson the characters, like the language, are direct, almost propositional, moral statements. Jonson's poetry analyzes his dystopian vision and roots the analysis in the language of learning. Shakespeare's poetry integrates his utopian vision by its suggestiveness.

The further point, however, is that *poesis* designates a moral as well as an aesthetic value. The rhetorical axes specify ways of uniting use with delight. In the same way, paradox is a moral and aesthetic value in Shaw and Stoppard and aphorism a moral and aesthetic value in sentimental as well as Restoration comedies. *Poesis* unifies language and law in Jonson just as it unifies language and metaphor in Shakespeare. It is, moreover, an aspect of our pleasure as well as perception.

One way of defining the pleasure in the rhetoric might be to suggest that the three terms I have chosen, *poesis, aphorism,* and *paradox,* parallel some of the structures that have traditionally been associated with the psychology of laughter. The three terms are not exhaustive, and it would be possible to extend the number, especially to deal with comedies in other languages. Those I have chosen, however, are particularly distinguishable from one another and might be considered extremes of comic capacities: for aggression, for inversion, and for integration.

Understandably, we separate the analysis of jokes and humor from the analysis of plays and comic structure. Many comedies are not funny, and many jokes in a play do not make it a comedy. One function of the rhetorical axes could be to suggest a conceptual unity of humor and comic form.

The idea of aggression appears fairly consistently in theories of laughter and comedy.[6] As Lady Sneerwell says in *School*

---

6. See especially Arthur Koestler, *The Act of Creation* (New York: Macmillan, 1964), pp. 51–63.

for Scandal, "There's no possibility of being witty without a little ill nature." If we can imagine the aggressive malice of certain jokes extended into comic form, we might discover the
Restoration comedy. The sometimes blatant malice could be
considered part of the rhetoric of the Restoration in the sense
that it is present in the attitude of many Restoration characters, present in the style and manner of the language, possibly
present in the playwrights, and definitely communicated to
an audience, whether that audience delights or disapproves.
Conversely, if we imagine aggression with an absolute absence of malice, we might find the humorless assertiveness
and righteousness of the sentimental comedies. The certainty
of moral stance in character and climate, the sermonizing language, the clarity of right and wrong communicated to the audience are aggressive in a particular way.

Inversion, or incongruity, is also a persistent term in theories of humor.[7] Whereas aggression is emotional, however,
inversion is perceptual. If we transfer the principle of inversion to a rhetoric of comedy, then *paradox* demonstrates the
same principle. Inversion and paradox both involve pleasure
in the perceptual principle. Through them we not only perceive possibilities and unlikely or incongruous pairings but
also gain a momentary sense of power over actuality. The very
perception leads to the imaginative power to manipulate or
change appearances. As the Feast of Fools temporarily inverts
the structure of social authority, so the paradoxes of Xeno temporarily invert logic and actuality, and as a result Tom Stoppard can point out, in *Jumpers*, that Saint Sebastian died of
fright. And Shaw can ironically maintain that salvation comes
through the munitions factory. The humor of the perception
combines with a sense of power over things as they are, even
if that power is no more than a fiction. My sense of paradox
goes beyond incongruity and beyond Koestler's idea of "bisociation," which is the intersection of contradictory codes or
matrices. I take paradox to be like the phenomenon of the
"Strange Loop," that is, the discovery of a contradiction that

7. Ibid., p. 35.

is both impossible and actual in a given system. Here is a logical Strange Loop: "The following sentence is false. The preceding sentence is true."[8]

Although related to the humor of bisociation, the paradox in this example emphasizes the self-enclosure of the form or system that creates it. Hence it is especially pertinent to questions of artifice/reality and fiction/truth and to the idea that reality comes into "meaning" in a fiction but is not identical to meaning; that in fiction we gain some measure of "power" over reality, but that power is ineffectual; that, like the paradox of the Strange Loop above, art is false and art is true.

Finally, theories of humor often focus on the cathartic function of laughter, suggesting that laughter integrates the human community and that laughter itself has a unifying or healing capacity. The cathartic effectiveness of laughter need not be the explosive release of excess emotions alone but might be, metaphorically, the creative explosion that unifies contradictory elements and embraces meaning and emotion as well. If we imagine such "present laughter" turning into a structure of comedy, we would find those plays that take "men as they are" through fictional situations and turn them into "men as they ought to be." This is the comic form in which desire is fulfilled. In the rhetoric of *poesis*, the world desires meaning through the word, and the word desires affective life from the world. It is not simply that all's well at the end of the play—in both Jonson and Shakespeare the sense of well-being is consistently laced with doubt—but that the mutual desires of world and word are satisfied: transience and persistence are one.

In these rhetorical elements we might locate a tripartite nature of delight. On the one hand, aggression, inversion, and integration are features of the performance elements of humor and laughter. As humor is evanescent and rises in the im-

---

8. Douglas R. Hofstadter, *Godel, Escher, Bach: An Eternal Golden Braid* (New York: Random House, Vintage Books, 1979), p. 21. Hofstadter concisely defines the "Strange Loop": "The 'Strange Loop' phenomenon occurs whenever, by moving upwards (or downwards) through levels of some hierarchical system, we unexpectedly find ourselves right back where we started" (p. 10).

mediate context of performance and audience, so it recalls the quality of the lampooning mode that is both delightful and corrective. On the other hand, we can discover ways in which these elements also inform comic structures. Pleasure in attack, pleasure in reversal, pleasure in unity: each can delight us in the ephemeral event. Yet we continually seek forms by which to make that ephemeral delight continue and try to justify our sometimes perverse and transient pleasures in the persistent terms of ethical structure. The mutual resistance of permanence and change, use and delight has created a history of comedy that cannot now escape our notice.

2

Shakespeare's *Poesis*
Use and Delight in Utopia

Dost thou think because thou art virtuous there shall be no
more cakes and ale?

Twelfth Night

Virtue and appetite, sobriety and revelry, respectability and
knavery, constancy and mutability: the opposition of moral
conditions like these defines a fundamental moral tension in
many comedies. Comedy often operates out of the collision of
desires and restrictions. And appetite in its various manifestations (lust, hunger, greed) is the bodily version of the moral
condition. It is the corporeal principle of desire, the irreduci-
ble human reality that comedy as a genre tends both to indulge and restrain. In the extreme and exaggerated form of
comedy, we have farce, in which the potential of the body's
appetites breaks the boundaries of realism to become the almost pure action of Appetite that consumes social or ethical
restraints in the delight of excess. In a more reduced form,
comedy brings the appetite into the drawing room with the
tea and toast or cucumber sandwiches that signify the larger
desires of human nature within the genteel domain of social
intercourse and the "higher love."

As a general statement about the action of comedy, we
might say that it customarily indulges human appetites—revels in them, so to speak—as it tries simultaneously to socialize
them. Corporeality and society are not mutually exclusive
spheres: from one perspective comedy is especially suited to
bringing the body into society. It aligns the isolated and iso-
lating attributes common to animals and humans (the body's
needs, its appetitive nature) in a functional social pattern.

Sometimes the realignment requires a modification of the appetites themselves, so that a character, either by reform or retribution, is brought "out of his humor" into a moral equilibrium. Ben Jonson's comedies usually punish the human
appetites with ridicule. Other comedies incorporate appetite
into their societies, which are then revitalized and rejuve-
nated by its vigor, as when the youthful lovers finally overcome all obstacles to their desires. The moral theme of appetite and virtue is an attenuation of a deeper tension between
chaos and order, between the potentially limitless hunger of
the biological being and the limitations imposed by the group
on the individual.

In comedy, this moral theme is at the heart of the contradiction in the form itself between indulgence and restriction. The
contradiction recalls an old comic dilemma: is comedy good
because it rewards virtue and punishes vice or because it re-
leases the individualized delight that is necessarily repressed
by society? One defense of comedy suggests that it teaches us
not what to imitate but what to avoid: we learn through the
example of ridicule. Another defense suggests that comedy is
a social cathartic: we celebrate our appetitive nature vicari-
ously, in a context without consequence, and delight in the
structure of revelry.[1] Comic misrule cleanses the society of
personal passions by indulging them in a controlled structure.

Toby Belch's rhetorical question to Malvolio in the epigraph
of this chapter suggests that puritanical virtue will never socialize appetite (cakes and ale).[2] The mere presence of virtue
does not guarantee any transformation or modification of appetite. The ethical structure represented by Malvolio's presence cannot restrain the revelry of Sir Toby and his friends. In
fact, that ethical structure invites the retribution of the revel-

---

1. The idea of the festive comedy as a structure for a social cathartic
"through release to clarification" is, of course, the basis for C. L. Barber,
Shakespeare's Festive Comedy (Princeton, N.J.: Princeton University Press,
1959).
   2. All quotations from *Twelfth Night* are from *The Riverside Shakespeare*, ed.
G. Blakemore Evans (Boston: Houghton Mifflin, 1974). Subsequent citations
will be given parenthetically in the text.

ers on its representative, and that retribution is the focus of much of our delight. It is too simple, really, to say that *Twelfth Night* offers a straightforward dialectic between virtue and revelry or sobriety and appetite, or that Shakespeare leads us to some "moral" sense of revelry.[3] The play is certainly like a revel. It celebrates in song, in dance, and sometimes in drunkenness. Malvolio is an obvious moral foil. But does the potential sympathy for Malvolio at the end of the play overtake the previous censure? The resolution of this kind of ethical question will inevitably rest in ethical taste: one can almost always make a play conform to one's own ethical attitudes, sympathies, and ideas of justice and retribution and fairness. Characters like Malvolio and Shylock are subject to constant revision, a revision that depends not so much on their function in the play as on an external perception of equity, fairness, or sympathy. Likewise, Katherina in *The Taming of the Shrew* is subject to currents of ethical taste that can shift and color her function in the comedy or at least turn the play toward specific commentary. Part of the problem in examining the moral structure of Shakespeare's comedy is that the moral themes are both obvious and transparent, as though we could see through them to the specific images and actions of the play or, conversely, as though we could see through the images and actions to the moral themes. Shakespeare makes his images moral and his morals imagistic, so that we do not know precisely what we are seeing or hearing; we know only that image and moral quality are both present.

The source of this phenomenon in Shakespeare can be defined by what I have called *poesis*. I include in this term the sense that language as a made thing, a fashioned object, is, at least in the Renaissance, a form of knowledge. It is the ground

---

3. See, for example, John Hollander, "*Twelfth Night* and the Morality of Indulgence," in *Discussions of Shakespeare's Romantic Comedy*, ed. Herbert Weil, Jr. (Boston: Heath, 1966), p. 120. Hollander usefully points out that Shakespeare "seems at any rate to have analyzed the dramatic and moral nature of feasting. . . . His analysis is schematized in Orsino's opening speech. The essential action of a revel is: To so surfeit the Appetite upon excess that it 'may sicken and so die.'"

of what Michel Foucault has called the preclassical *episteme*. Language is still joined to its objects; there is no separation of words and things, because the world is knowable by the relations of things, by analogy, by "convenience" or proximity, by the conjunction of visible signs and invisible objects. In this field of *episteme*, words belong to things as part of their nature; they are not only signs. Nature is whole; it rounds back on itself and can therefore be known by a system of correspondence. Foucault says that the idea of the microcosm is fundamental to this form of knowledge.

> As a *category of thought*, it applies the interplay of duplicated resemblances to all the realms of nature; it provides all investigation with an assurance that everything will find its mirror and its macrocosmic justification on another and larger scale; it affirms, inversely, that the visible order of the highest spheres will be found reflected in the darkest depths of the earth.[4]

This epistemological ground necessarily includes a mixture of "magic and erudition" because the knowledge of an object consists of a compilation of all that is seen, heard, or written of it.[5] *Poesis*, as I define it, is thus not only a signifier of a world but also an interpreter/creator of a world. Poetic language gives a location to the "natural" correspondence between words and things, images and moral qualities. If the cosmos can be understood on the basis of analogy, resemblances, and correspondence, *poesis* can ground an analogue in a single word, illuminating the whole by the part. It is through *poesis* that a moral theme can be traced by images.

In *Twelfth Night*, for example, the moral/imagistic ground is established immediately, beginning with Orsino's opening speech that equates music, food, and love. The equation develops through the play; it proliferates. From the beginning we collect references to food and drink, appetite, music, love, and sea. The images and references become repetitious, like a musical motif. To put it another way, they become ency-

4. Michel Foucault, *The Order of Things: An Archaeology of the Human Sciences* (New York: Random House, Vintage Books, 1970), p. 31.

5. Ibid., pp. 32–40.

clopedic, as though the play were compiling all the possible
variations on the equation. Orsino's appetite for love is ready
to surfeit, but it is insatiable; his love is as capacious and in-
constant as the sea; he is drunk and ready to sicken and so die
with love. Sir Toby makes the oceanic theme physical: he has
an unquenchable thirst for ale and will drink toasts to Olivia
"as long as there's passage in my throat and drink in Illyria"
(1.3.39–40). Malvolio, too, is "sick of self-love"; he "tastes
with a distemper'd appetite" (1.5.90–91). The repeated references to appetite, sickness, drink, delirium have little to do
with the action or structure of the play but a great deal to do
with the moral world of the play. Language centers the action
and interprets it through a specific set of images and qualities.
Moreover, the play compiles an encyclopedia or natural history of the connection between appetite, sickness, drunkenness, and love through its characters and its language. The
moral anatomy of this world is not in the structure of the action as much as in the collection of analogies.

Illyria is a watery world. Within that world, the court of Orsino and the household of Olivia are two self-enclosed mon-
uments of self-deception. As many people have already noticed, the dominant images in *Twelfth Night* are of fluidity: the
sea, drink, tears, water, ale, urine, rain.[6] In addition to Toby's
drink, there are Olivia's tears; there is Feste's remark, "I'm for
all waters" (4.2.63); there is Orsino's love, "all as hungry as the
sea" (2.4.100); and the play ends with the song whose refrain
is "the rain it raineth every day." To this fluid environment are
opposed images of constancy and confinement. "I would
have men of such constancy put to sea" (2.4.76), says Feste of
Orsino. When Feste is called a "dry fool," he replies that
"drink and good counsel will amend; for give the dry fool
drink, then is the fool not dry" (1.5.43–44). Malvolio's physical imprisonment corresponds to the rigid nature of his virtue.
Similarly, Olivia lives in a self-imposed confinement of grief,
and Orsino is bound by the chains of love. Viola's image of

6. Hollander, "Morality of Indulgence," p. 131.

"Patience on a monument" is one of the most striking examples of constancy in the play. Shakespeare's images define the moral scope of his plays by defining the physical characteristics of an image or set of images. In the reiterated references to both water and confinement he defines a moral system without resorting to sermons. The images are emblematic, much like the medieval or Renaissance illustrations that both teach the unschooled and delight the scholar. The advantage of the emblem is that it functions both as a sign for a moral problem and as a concrete instance of that problem. It is at once a specific image and an abstruse puzzle.

T. S. Eliot called such images the "suggestive" or "evocative" aspects of Shakespeare's language,[7] but they are also self-evident images. They bear content that is subject to interpretation, but they do not "interpret themselves." The images are significative, but they are also instances of knowing. An image of "fluidity" is an instance of "fluidity," not as an object specifically but as a quality. Because Shakespeare's images pervade his plays and fill them not with objects but with qualities, he creates a "rhetorical" world in qualitative terms.

The metaphoric potential of an image leads us, as audiences, to build bridges from the qualities of the images to the qualities of a "world" and hence begin to attach moral qualities to the actions of characters. In Illyria, for example, we see Orsino's love "all as hungry as the sea" and begin to attach moral qualities to a human situation, arriving at both a "character" for Orsino and a moral "problem" for the play. Through similes, images, or analogies, we begin to locate the problem indicated by the *poesis* as a problem of character or situation. Orsino's problem thus seems to be a languishing love and an appetite for melancholy. In his first speech, he seems to be asking for an end to his appetite for love, hoping that if he feeds it, it might die. But like all lovers who enjoy the exquisite torture of being denied, he is also in love with denial, or at least with the agitation and excitement that denial creates.

7. T. S. Eliot, *Elizabethan Essays* (New York: Haskell House, 1964), p. 66.

> For such as I am, all true lovers are,
> Unstaid and skittish in all motions else,
> Save in the constant image of the creature
> That is belov'd.
>
> (2.4.17–20)

From such speeches we begin to create a "being." We begin to say that Orsino "is" such and such a kind of person. He "is" a romantic, lugubrious lover, transfixed by the image of perfection, a self-contained monument to romantic love.

When Viola tells Orsino her image of someone in love, we see different qualities:

> she pin'd in thought,
> And with a green and yellow melancholy
> She sate like Patience on a monument,
> Smiling at grief.
>
> (2.4.112–15)

The speech not only describes an abstract virtue but also adds that virtue to our sense of Viola's complexity as "character"; furthermore it comments on the static quality of Orsino's love. In the play—above and beyond what the characters say about themselves—Viola is all activity, moving between court and household. Orsino is a passive lover for all his agitation. His love is an agitation in a static state; Viola's love is a constant, a monument of patience in action. We sense here, then, a Viola who has an "inside" and an "outside": constancy or patience "within," action and deeds "without." Orsino's condition causes him to mistake the appropriate object of love. Viola's condition enables her to function in the realm of actuality. The qualitative contrast between Viola's love and Orsino's is thus generated by language and transferred to character and situation. In moral or psychological terms, we could say that agitated stasis and transfixed activity form the paradox of love in this play. The insatiable, self-consuming love of Orsino's appetite immobilizes him; the antidote for his immobility is the constancy and patience of Viola's active love. We extrapolate moral and emotional value as well as psychological complexity from the capacity of language to design without designating. From the total pattern or design that the language creates, we derive a value-laden world of characters and actions. Characters locate contrasting values for us, but some difficulties arise when we try to judge the moral meaning of the play on the basis of the characters' values. The "problems" of *Twelfth Night* are not solved by right ethical decisions or by the punishment of malefactors. The opposition either of Orsino's languishing love and Viola's active love, for example, or of virtue and appetite as a moral theme is not subjected to judgment. In neither opposition is one element really preferable to the other, for both are realities of the larger condition of the play. Sir Toby's question to Malvolio does not deny virtue, nor does it mean that the play speaks only for cakes and ale and the virtue of revelry. Such a simplistic ethical dialectic belongs to an analytic vision of society and value. Shakespeare has a synthetic vision: he does not necessarily deny the possibility of ethical choice or rightness but finds ways to implicate various possibilities in the unity of the whole.

If we try to choose between the value of appetite and the value of virtue, for example, we impose a judgment on the play that the play does not call for, one that in fact diminishes the inclusiveness of possibilities. Suppose we try to divide the play between virtuous characters and actions and appetitive ones. We will find not a division but a range of virtues with various characteristics. Olivia, to be sure, is a "virtuous maid, daughter of a count," but her hunger blinds her to the "reality" of Cesario's identity. Malvolio is virtuous in his way; he is in fact virtuous to the point of self-righteousness, and the extreme makes him ridiculous. Orsino is "appetitive" yet is clearly one of the romantic centers of the play. Sir Toby is insatiable yet affirms the value, if not the virtue, of the revel. We discover not an ethical dialectic between virtue and appetite but a catalogue of the kinds and degrees of each. The very inclusiveness of this "world" makes certain ethical questions inappropriate.

The moral questions that arise over the gulling of Malvolio, for instance, indicate the extent to which we presume both the presence of an ethical question and the "corrective" nature of comedy. We often seek a moral justification for that mean treatment of Malvolio at the hands of the clowns. He is, of course, too puritanical, too full of pride and self-deception, too much a spoilsport, and too rigidly virtuous. He deserves his comeuppance. On the other hand, he is merely doing his duty to Olivia; the rogues of the household are out of control and morally decadent. Their game suggests a deep cruelty. From either perspective we are passing a sympathetic and ethical judgment: and either our sympathy creates an ethical system or our ethical system creates our sympathy.

The "dramatic" answer, of course, is that Malvolio "works." His punishment is an aspect of the play's comedy, and we can maintain the possibility of an ethical attitude (he receives his just deserts or is cruelly treated) but must take into account the aesthetic perspective, or the purely "formal" aspect, of comic punishment. Such punishment is part of the performance pleasure in the tradition of comedy, an attenuation of the old "lampooning mode." The source of that pleasure may be our own latent aggressiveness, which we would rather not acknowledge, but at the very least we are asked to momentarily suspend judgment in favor of comic pleasure.

I do not mean to suggest that there is no moral residue in Malvolio. He deserves his punishment, but at the same time that punishment is malicious. Although we would hate to see him revenged, his final cry for revenge is justified. His departure threatens to spoil the spirit of the final moment. Like Shylock, he is a problem character. Like Jaques and Shylock, he leaves a trace element of moral ambiguity. Yet that, too, is an aspect of inclusiveness in Shakespeare's moral scheme. The corrective or analytic comedy leaves no moral residue. It is far more efficient in its clarification of virtue and vice. The comic world of Shakespeare is less efficient in its retribution than a Jonsonian world but perhaps more completely satisfying.

The illusion of a complete world in *Twelfth Night* is created by thematic pattern. We feel that Illyria is homogeneous in spite of its diversity because its inhabitants and their actions all revolve around a structural theme. Because the actions of Sir Toby and his friends have no direct effect on the actions or events of the romantic couples, some people feel that in strictly narrative terms this is a divided play. But Olivia and Viola are no less exempt from appetite as love than Toby is exempt from appetite as drink. Indeed, Olivia's love for Cesario is a version of the delirium that Viola feels for Orsino and that Toby exhibits in his perpetual drunkenness: they are all at least "one draught above heat." The sameness in their conditions is distinguished only by degree and proportion, with the result that degree and proportion constitute the normative order of the world of the play, above and beyond the specific ethical content of characters or action.

One of the distinguishing elements of the "utopian" comedy is the sense of place that it creates, the sense of a space in which actions are qualitatively coherent though logically or ethically inconsistent. The thematic space encloses characters and maintains some autonomy from them. We know, for example, as soon as Viola's brother Sebastian enters Illyrian space that a symmetry is complete and the conclusion is inevitable, just as we know that when Oliver enters the forest of Arden, his conversion is necessary and probable. Probability, however, depends on the convention of the artifice, not on its verisimilitude. The traditional form that celebrates the capacities for transformation through artifice is the pastoral, and Shakespeare's comedies are rarely far from the pastoral scheme. Illyria is not exactly Arcadia, yet as a locale it has the pastoral attributes that stop time, confuse identities, allow for the indulgence of love and celebration, and remind us that there is death, even in utopia.

The sense that place can be distinguishable from character identifies Shakespeare's utopian perspective. The fictional "world" effects "character" more than characters create the world. Choice and action in Shakespeare's characters are not the agents of development and change. Orsino does not learn the nature of true love any more than Sir Toby learns moderation. It is not, finally, left to Viola to resolve the confusions of identity. Resolution comes quite specifically through the agent of time, which is another way of saying through the impersonal action of the narrative.

> O time, thou must untangle this, not I,
> It is too hard a knot for me t'untie.
>   (2.3.40–41)

The invocation to Time addresses the impersonal elements in the structure of the artifice. Time changes the situations of the characters, but it does not alter their ethical status. A Jonsonian play, by way of contrast, does not ask time to untangle the knots of complication; it asks only that the character conform to a projected moral order or be punished for lack of conformity. In Jonson, an ethical logic determines the "quality" of the world. This determination may be entirely appropriate for an ethical diagnosis of human nature, but it binds Jonson's world to the logical unities of time and place.

In Shakespeare the causality of action is not bound to temporal logic and sequence but to the thematic logic of the fictional space. That space has a magic quality because it is free of temporal causality in the same way that poetry is free of the temporal logic of discourse. Illyria is an ideal world not because characters are morally perfect or because wishes are fulfilled but because it coheres as a fiction. If we transfer our habit of making ethical judgments about characters (appropriate in a Jonsonian world) to Shakespeare's, we tend to say Olivia "learns" the limits of grief, or Orsino "learns" the true value of love, or Malvolio "learns" through punishment about excess. But because the play is not structured on the logic of ethical choices, Shakespeare appears to have no moral program for the appetitive nature of humans in love. As a result, we "learn" more about love and appetite in humans than about humans in love.

The distinction is important because it keeps us from looking too closely for either psychological or moral consistency in Shakespeare's comic characters. Shakespeare is able to objectify elements of human experience as an almost autonomous arena in which characters operate. The fictional world of theme and artifice, not a standard of ethical probity, creates the comic norm. And that norm is a matter of proportion and decorum, which are the province of the artist.

Twelfth Night designates artifice as a norm through the character of Feste. In her reprimand to Malvolio, Olivia implicitly links morality to artistry, suggesting that generosity and a free disposition give one a right sense of proportion.

> O, you are sick of self-love, Malvolio, and taste with a distemper'd appetite. To be generous, guiltless, and of a free disposition, is to take those things for bird-bolts that you deem cannon bullets. There is no slander in an allow'd fool, though he do nothing but rail; nor no railing in a known discreet man, though he do nothing but reprove.
>
> (1.5.90–96)

With a strictly ethical norm, we judge Malvolio as a "bad" character, who comes straight from a Jonsonian comedy for punishment, and Feste as a "good" character, generous and guiltless. But as Olivia suggests in her speech, ethical order is less a matter of content than of proportion. Malvolio's lack is as much aesthetic as it is moral. The allowed fool, like the allowed fiction, is exempt from the charge of slander. The artful fool, unlike the discreet man, knows that the difference between bird-bolts and cannon bullets, between fiction and reality, is a matter of proportion and taste.

Both Olivia and Viola are "normative" characters in an ethical sense: they "are" virtuous, deserving, honorable, and reasonably sensible. But the play does not rest on the trials or proofs of their virtues any more than on the proofs of Toby's drunken antics. The ethical constitution of the romantic figures may satisfy us, but those characters are simply part of the narrative "generator," so to speak. They move us along to a fitting narrative conclusion, but that conclusion is no more than we expect. In addition, some of our interest in the lovers as characters comes from the differences between them and the pattern they create as varying instances of the appetite/

virtue/love theme. That theme creates an ethical space, a qualitative location for the action of the play. But Feste is at the center of this ethical space, in the eye of the storm, not because he is an "ethical" character but because he is the one figure who perceives the totality of the action.

In strict ethical terms, Feste is an anomalous presence. If this were a morality play with a morality structure, he might well be seen as a Vice figure. But *Twelfth Night* reaches beyond a simple moral dialectic, and Feste has none of the perverse antic disposition of a character like Mosca in *Volpone*. He has, however, some of the same freedom. Moreover, in Feste we can see how vestiges of a morality structure or corrective comedy can open out on the larger vistas of Shakespeare's comedy. Feste has no "character" per se, no project, no apparent needs, no attachments, yet he is a crucial spokesman for the play. I do not mean he is a spokesman for Shakespeare's intent, any more than the other characters are. They all take their place in the scheme of the whole. But Feste is an oddity. He is a dramatis persona without any desires. He moves freely between Olivia's household and Orsino's court but is always, somehow, in his own place. His commentary is specific but also impersonal. His humor is light and playful, but he carries with him the reminder of death. Moving unattached through the play, he sings songs that honor both the *carpe diem* aspect of love ("Come and kiss me sweet and twenty") and its deathly aspect ("Sad true lover never find my grave to weep there"). Feste embodies the moral themes of the pastoral: the interpenetration of time and timelessness, love and death, life and art. Like the gravestone in Arcadia, he recalls "Et in Arcadia Ego," but he does not diminish the momentary pleasures of the art form that celebrates desire, passion, appetite, love. His presence rather heightens that momentary celebration and makes it more valuable because of its fragility. He combines the pleasure and pain of finity that is the particular domain of the clown/comedian/performer.

DUKE: There's for thy pains.
CLOWN: No pains, sir, I take pleasure in singing, sir.

DUKE: I'll pay thy pleasure then.
CLOWN: Truly, sir, and pleasure will be paid, one time or
another.

(2.4.67–71)

Feste is an emblematic character for this comedy. *Twelfth Night* oscillates precariously between what we commonly call the two phases of Shakespeare's canon. Even as it is comic and celebratory and directed toward the happy alignment of couples, it also foreshadows the disintegration of innocence in *The Merchant of Venice, All's Well That Ends Well, Measure for Measure* and *Troilus and Cressida.* Feste foreshadows the darker ironies of these comedies, but the action of *Twelfth Night* leads to the happy and uncomplicated alignment of couples. Pleasure will be paid, but in the meantime there is song and celebration. Feste is both a reveler and an ironic commentator. More than that, however, he demonstrates in an extreme way how Shakespeare keeps characters in proportion to his themes. Lacking either a specific motive or a personal drive in the action of the play, Feste is the internal ironic voice of the play speaking directly to us. His distance from the other characters coincides with their full acceptance of him in their midst: he functions both inside and outside the play. He is the singer, the performer, the poet who keeps revelry and irony in the proper degree. He is the emblem of comic pleasure always aware of the limitations and cost of that pleasure. As the singer-poet represents *poesis,* so Feste locates the analogic proportion between the transitory/permanent nature of love and appetite in performance and the transitory/permanent nature of life. Moreover, Feste signals us that language itself both creates and disintegrates. "A sentence is but a chev'ril glove to a good wit" (3.1.12). Feste, as he tells Viola, is not Lady Olivia's fool but her "corrupter of words."

Poesis lies midway between the usefulness of language as fixed and cognitive and the delight of language as transient and suggestive. Words both bind meaning and loose it on the world, but the bonds are not absolute, and as Viola says, "They that dally nicely with words may quickly make them wanton"(3.1.14–15). The bonds of words and things, such as "my sister's name" and "my sister," have been "disgrac'd," so Feste "would therefore my sister had no name" since "to dally with that word might make my sister wanton." We are amused to think that the imaginary bond between the word and the thing (such as sister) might be so effective. It is less amusing to consider that the "thing" might have no effect, that is, effective meaning, on the word; but if the bond does not truly exist, then the loss is mutual.

The words of the play create a cognitive world of qualities: love and appetite, as hungry as the sea. Language brings into being what never existed, yet we still feel "loss" at the end of the play with Feste's "But that's all one, our play is done." Our pleasure in language is only partially derived from the illusion of a world as an "object" created by words. That pleasure, in Shakespeare's *poesis*, comes from language that is not identical to reality and that allows us respite from actuality. We pay for that pleasure with a sense of loss, but that very cost makes the experience acute. Moreover, Feste as fool and clown embodies that experience, for he is the emblem of revelry and death conjoined. It is Feste who, in celebration, continually reminds us that death is still a reality, that pleasure will be paid, that youth's a stuff will not endure. In the revels scene at Olivia's house, Sir Toby sings, "But I will never die"; Feste answers, singing, "Sir Toby there you lie"; Malvolio adds, speaking, "This is much credit to you" (2.3.106–8), either as a sarcastic comment on all their tomfoolery or as an acknowledgment of the truth in Feste's statement. Shakespeare's perspective is inclusive and ironic because it recognizes the place and function of death and finity in the idealized ethical structure of love and marriage. The development of the narrative toward an ethical structure is countered by the loss and disintegration inherent in performative transience: but loss as much as structure is a source of delight.

The comic structure gives a particular direction to the thematic consistency. As a theme, that is, love and time are most purely developed in the lyric voice and the emotional experience of the single poet. Taken out of the singular and personal voice and brought into the social context of comedy, the theme is modified and qualified. Comedy socializes the singularity and isolation of a personal emotion, but it thereby threatens to alter the experience. The individual can no longer dwell alone with his feeling. In many ways, Orsino is not a member of the comic community in *Twelfth Night*. He remains an isolated, melancholy lover until the very end of the play. If the pressure of isolation becomes too great, love can lead to tragedy, as it does for Othello. One can easily imagine, however, that were Othello to bring his jealous passion into the community, to share it with his society, not just with Iago, it would quickly appear to be a comic passion. Because he holds it in, his passion consumes him. The dark side of love in *Twelfth Night*, its deathly aspect, threatens to turn to irony. But because it is activated by the social world of Illyria, it remains comic. If only consuming and appetitive love were found there, Illyria might become the horrific and ironic world of *Troilus and Cressida*. But the passion of love's appetite is social and belongs to the community at large in Illyria. The paradoxes of love's change and love's permanence are set in motion there and cannot come to rest in either the *carpe diem* of celebration or the irony of death. Appetite and virtue, change and permanence are the moral and thematic boundaries of a social world.

In Shakespeare's utopian perspective, appetite is not restricted or restrained by society. Rather, it is found to have its own natural cycle of ebb and flow, desire and surfeit. It is a permanent fixture in constant flux. Sir Toby's appetite for cakes and ale is the corporeal manifestation of appetite that no amount of virtue will eliminate. In this Renaissance world of correspondences, resemblances, and analogies, that corporeal appetite is a likeness of the universal paradox of permanence and change and the continual progress toward the death of desire in the acquisition of its object. One can revel in an appetite because the appetite will die a natural death. *Twelfth Night* can celebrate delight not to escape from the reality of death and change but to acknowledge the presence of death and change in delight. The play exhibits the potential purity of comic delight in the context of an impure reality. Only Feste is aware of the impurity, perhaps, but his presence reveals the importance of revelry even in a world where death is inevitable. Because he tells us that pleasure will be paid, that "the rain it raineth every day," and that "youth's a stuff will not endure," we experience more poignantly the delight in the outcome of the comic structure and still witness the universal principles that belong to that structure, principles of time and timelessness, motion and stasis. Feste presents the context in which revelry and delight are useful. He helps the play to signal both that all human experience is transitory and subject to change and decay and that sometimes in imaginary structures we can experience the satisfaction of an appetite.

3

Jonson's *Poesis*
Use and Delight in Dystopia

Quid sit Comoedia? . . . *Imitatio vitae, Speculum consuetudinis,*
Imago veritatis.

Every Man out of His Humour

The familiar refrain that comedy is the imitation of life, the
mirror of manners, and the image of reality had become a
commonplace long before the Renaissance. A persistent tradition from Cicero through Donatus into the Renaissance distinguishes comedy as the genre of public and private behavior
that teaches what to practice and what to avoid. According to
this tradition, comedy is "useful" in the pragmatic sense of
the word.

Ben Jonson uses the Ciceronian formula quoted in the epigraph of this chapter during an exchange between the internal
commentators of *Every Man out of His Humour*, Mitis and Cordatus.[1] In the middle of act 3 Mitis worries that the crowd will
find fault with the argument of the play—will be unhappy
with the story, in other words—and will bring their objections
against the author before Mitis has a chance to understand the
play. Mitis suspects the audience would prefer another kind
of play, "as of a duke to be in love with a countess, and that
countess to be in love with the duke's son, and the son to love
the ladies waiting maid: some such cross-wooing, with a

---

1. All quotations from *Every Man out of His Humour* and *Every Man in His
Humour* are from *Ben Jonson*, vol. 3, ed. C. H. Herford and Percy Simpson (Oxford: Clarendon Press, 1927). I have, however, taken liberties with the text in
capitalizing only the beginnings of lines and in changing *u* to *v* to provide
modern spellings of some words. Subsequent citations from the play will be
given parenthetically in the text.

clown to their servingman" (3.6.196–99). Cordatus, "the author's friend; a man inly acquainted with the scope and drift of his plot; of a discreet, and understanding judgment," replies that unless some wise member of the audience can improve on Cicero's definition of comedy, it would be best to remember that definition: "a thing throughout pleasant, and ridiculous, and accommodated to the correction of manners" (3.6.207–9).

Jonson is defending his play against those who want only to see wishes fulfilled—against those who want Shakespeare. Romantic comedy may please an audience, but it will neither reflect human nature nor teach the audience to know themselves. And if a comedy is to instruct with the aim of correcting, it must first reflect the reality of "men as they are," not as they would be. It must not indulge in fantasy, romance, and cross-wooing. It is clear that Jonson relies heavily on tradition as the source of his authority in his comedies, yet he uses that authority not for the structure it suggests, or for the limits it provides, or out of any insecurity about his own authority. He uses the tradition, or he is *in* the tradition, because it coincides with his own purpose and temperament and style, not because he somehow lacks the imagination to break away. We often feel sorry for Jonson, I think, not only because he is not Shakespeare but also because we think he is confined by the weight of his learning and burdened by classical definitions. It is more appropriate, however, to see how Jonson turns the tradition to his own ends and how he feels free to modify it. As he says in *Every Man out of His Humour*, the neoclassic rules were not delivered *"ab initio"* but are continually modified by the augmentations or deletions of authors writing for their own times. Jonson claims the same liberty and license to heighten his invention and refuses to be "tied to those strict and regular forms, which the niceness of a few . . . would thrust upon us" (Induction, ll. 268–70). The classical tradition suits Jonson because its terms are moral, concrete, and practical and because it allows the attitude of the author to surface in the objects of ridicule.

Every Man out of His Humour is a helpful place to begin discussion because whatever it lacks in persistent comic effectiveness it makes up for in the clear unity of theory and comic action. It is a play that explains itself theoretically as it goes along.

Comedy and comic theory in this play combine structurally in the elimination of barriers between the audience and the play. Perhaps it would be more accurate to say that the barriers become mobile and temporary, erected for convenience during the play proper, struck out for the commentary by Mitis and Cordatus, who act as our critical intermediaries. Throughout the play they serve as theorists, explaining not only the moral action but the purpose of comedy. These two characters make manifest the generally latent capacity of comic satire to penetrate theatrical barriers so that the audience, told the opinions of the author directly, is implicated in the moral postures of the comic satire. Yet Mitis and Cordatus themselves are intermediaries and serve less as the voice of Ben Jonson the playwright than as negotiators between Jonson and his potential critics. They imagine objections and answer them and hence are the voices of an imaginary critical audience. One of them is the author's friend, who knows intimately the author's purpose; the other is an innocent spectator, with neither action nor "character," according to the description in the list of dramatis personae. These two characters allow the play a rational self-consciousness. They place the play on the grid of a rational system of theory, and they make sure that the audience, play, and playwright are all working in that system. Unlike the Vice figure of the play, Asper, who also functions in the realms of both play and audience, the function of these two characters is to display a theoretical grid.

A character with ambivalent status is a consistent comic convention. These two characters, however, give extra theoretical distance to the moral intent of the play. That moral intent is described passionately by Asper in his exchange with Mitis and Cordatus. Mitis makes an appeal for calm, but Asper's zeal is overwhelming, and we see that the passion of his vision is the deeper impulse toward correction.

> Who is so patient of this impious world,
> That he can checke his spirit, or reine his tongue?
> Or who hath such a dead unfeeling sense,
> That heavens horrid thunders cannot wake?
> To see the earth, crackt with the weight of sinne,
> Hell gaping under us, and o're our heads
> Black rav'nous ruine, with her sail-stretcht wings,
> Ready to sinke us downe and cover us.
> Who can behold such prodigies as these,
> And have his lips seal'd up? not I: my language
> Was never ground into such oyly colours,
> To flatter vice and daube iniquitie.
>   (Induction, ll. 4–15)

This apocalyptic rage might well be Jonson's own. The zealous vision of heaven and earth, hell and ruination accounts for the reforming spirit. The zeal is perhaps humorous, but it nonetheless speaks eloquently of the range of Jonson's dystopian vision. This is not a vision of a petty social reform movement but of a fundamental rupture, of the earth cracking with the weight of sin, the mouth of hell gaping, and heaven's thunderous doom impending. Certainly we do not want to take it as Jonson's personal "vision" of the world. As Alvin Kernan points out in *The Cankered Muse*, Jonson goes to some effort "to make clear that the character of the satirist is a mask which an author assumes for the purpose of making a lasting impression on the world he is attacking."[2] The fervor of the satirist is not ordinary social concern. It occasionally has the desperation of one who sees the evil of the world prospering and proliferating absolutely, like the consuming beasts of our science fiction who spread death and destruction in an orgy of unquenchable appetite. Sin multiplies, spreads like the plague, infects manners and judgment, deforms the times.

> Well I will scourge those apes;
> And to these courteous eyes oppose a mirrour,
> As large as is the stage, whereon we act:
> Where they shall see the times deformitie

2. Alvin Kernan, *The Cankered Muse: Satire of the English Renaissance* (New Haven, Conn.: Yale University Press, 1959), p. 137.

Anatomiz'd in every nerve and sinnew,
With constant courage, and contempt of fear.
(Induction, ll. 117–22)

Jonson does not want to suggest helpfully how things
might be better; he wants to scourge human bestiality, eradi-
cate sin, clear out infested corners. If evil is absolute, only the
wrath of the righteous, the courage of the warrior, and the
acid bath of comic ridicule can effectively fight it. The theory
of comic correction is no nice abstraction for Jonson. It is
rather a passionate polemic that bears an apocalyptic burden.
In this vision, evil or sin is an endlessly regenerating monster
that duplicates itself everywhere. In fact, the sameness of sin
informs Jonsonian comedy—sin is identical to itself no matter
what the particular instance or manifestation. Unlike Shakespeare's comedies, Jonson's have no mitigating circumstances, no qualified errors or character, no degree or proportion
in values. Moral structure is absolute in that moral faults are
singularly themselves, not aspects of multifaceted characters
or situations. The faults, indeed, create the situations. One
way to see the difference between the integration of values in
Shakespeare and the dialectic of values in Jonson is to locate
the differences in the site of the ideal.

Value and the ideal are the manifest content of Shakespeare's romantic comedy. His plays are occasions for the enactment of a mythic norm, and wishes are fulfilled in the
hoped-for manner. The plays themselves are the site of the
"ideal," for clearly such a world can exist only imaginarily and
in an aesthetically designed fiction. In the actions of romance,
every Jack shall have his Jill despite all adversity, disguise,
jealousy, shipwrecks or banishment, winter or rough weather.
Characters and themes derive specificity from images of the
site and its qualities: the sea in *Twelfth Night*, the forest in *As
You Like It*, the moon in *A Midsummer Night's Dream*. Shakespearean images qualify and give quality to the play's action,
centering the plays pictorially and thematically, and holding
value in the immediate and concrete situation of the play. In
Shakespeare's fictional hierarchy lovers maintain their place

in an order: Silvius has Phebe, Touchstone has Audrey, Celia finds Oliver, and Rosalind finds Orlando. There is no unrequited passion for a partner of an inappropriate class. Part of the satisfaction in the romance form and the pastoral pattern comes out of the combination of range and containment, of diversity centered on a thematic axis. It is not so much that we get to know and like the particular characters of the pastoral/romance but that we know and like their place and function in the order of the world. The pattern of the romantic comedies and the late romances creates an ideal structure (both social and psychic), allowing within that structure for degrees of virtue and vice, wisdom and error. The pattern permits a great range of types—rustics, shepherds, dukes, wealthy heiresses, merchants, pedants, lost children, middle-class husbands and wives—the mixing, in short, of kings and clowns. The mixture gives the illusion of a wide and deep perspective, with shepherds in the distance, the city in the middle ground, lovers in the foreground, and the occasional Jaques or Malvolio as "blots" on the landscape to provide the contrasting reminder of imperfection. The world is both centered and extensive because in Shakespeare's *poesis* the moral space of language is both perfect and mutable, whole and contingent. It appears to have both temporal and spatial dimension.

In Jonson, the sense of dimension is flattened, but not because Jonson had a limited perspective, lacked subtlety, or had a failure of vision. Jonson's comedy is an instrument in the service of a distant ideal; it is his sword of righteousness in a corrupt world. He flattens and enlarges moral problems to make them self-evident, for he is interested less in the wholeness of the fictional world than in the corruption in the real one. The site of the ideal is outside the satirical play; at best it is an abstraction or an idea of a place without sin or disease. Divided from this unspoken and unseen idea, Jonson's world is a fallen and evil place.

Jonson's *poesis* does not project toward the ideal. His language is deictic. By contrast, Shakespeare's is metaphoric. I do not mean simply that Shakespeare uses metaphor but that he offers a pattern of qualities or attributes that do not specifically attach to objects. He relies on the metaphoric habit of the reader/audience to "carry over" or project qualities into an imaginary world. The result in Shakespeare is that the word is freed from the object and, playfully independent, dallies and grows "wanton," as Feste says. Jonson's word, conversely, is bound to objects, and attributes are consistently attached to things, in effect imprisoning the world in the word. The world in Shakespeare is a projection or displacement away from language into a nonexistent utopia; our sense of dimension comes from the distance between the corporeality of the language and the "elsewhere" of the projected world. The world in Jonson is concretely manifest in words; meaning is bound and referential. The word and world are a united corporeality, and hence there is no sense of dimension, no gap of metaphor. For Jonson the satirist, language is a weapon, not a toy. The site of the satirical plays of Jonson, then, is a site of almost pure materiality. Kernan describes the profusion of material objects as characteristic of the satiric scene: "The scene is . . . choked with things: ostentatious buildings and statuary, chariots, sedan-chairs, clothes, books, food, horses, dildoes, luxurious furnishings, gin bottles, wigs. Pick up any major satiric work and open it at random and the immediate effect is one of disorderly profusion."[3] The binding of word and thing is the linguistic version of the physical scene; indeed, it creates the physical scene. The source of delight in this language is not its suggestiveness but its material power.

T. S. Eliot revived the admiration for Jonson in this century. He was well aware that Jonson suffered for his lack of dimensionality and his apparent superficiality, especially in comparison with Shakespeare's wide design. But Eliot insisted that the "poetry of the surface" has to be studied thoughtfully, not emotionally, "for to deal with the surface of life, as Jonson dealt with it, is to deal so deliberately that we too must deliberate, in order to understand."[4] Jonson's poetry is concrete, specific to a situation, explicit in its moral position, and cer-

---

3. Ibid., p. 8.
4. T. S. Eliot, *Elizabethan Essays* (New York: Haskell House, 1964), p. 66.

tainly unemotional. There is more to the comparison of Jonson and Shakespeare, however, than the sense that Shakespeare arouses "swarms of inarticulate feelings" and that Jonson appeals to the mind. The poetry of the surface in Jonson delights in its own instrumentality and materiality.

> But it may well be call'd poore mortals Plague;
> For like a pestilence it doth infect
> The houses of the braine: first it begins
> Solely to worke upon the fantasie,
> Filling her seat with such pestiferous aire,
> As soone corrupts the judgement, and from thence,
> Sends like contagion to the memorie,
> Still each of other catching the infection
>   (1.4.206–13)

This description of the action of the humors from *Every Man in His Humour* suggests how well the representation of the humors suits the poetry of the surface. In general, that is, Jonson needs a language of and for the body. It is not so much that the plays are "about" humors in the body as that they are centered in the concrete materiality of the body and its appetites. The body is the location of obdurate materiality and of the biological and appetitive nature of man that is morally unformed. Moral nature gives the body form. We "read" moral nature from the body of the individual, and the body, then, is the text. Language in a speech like the one quoted above explains the corporeal text in moral terms and applies moral criticism to the evidence of the body.

Although *Twelfth Night* is concerned thematically with appetite, the characters seem distinct from the theme. Jonson's characters, on the other hand, are totally identified with their bodily/moral appetites; and they reiterate their singular obsessions endlessly. The sense of a universal disease, of corruption and plague is thematically consistent in Jonson, as though not only his characters but he himself were obsessed. Diseases are located in the body, yet they are morally conceived. The Jonsonian disease causes no physical pain, for it is not a disorder of feelings but of moral equilibrium. The result is a flattening or compression of time and space and the dimensions of reality into the dimensionless site of a moral concept. Time and place are formal unities in Jonson because they provide the framework for moral outrage. Time is only sequential. It has no depth because events follow each other by the logic of causality in moral faults. Place is simply a backdrop, without dimension. There is no sense of space in Jonson's world because the site of action is in the moral corporeality of his characters. The total corruption of the Jonsonian world leaves no room for shading, coloration, depth, or distance. Nor is there an opportunity for time to unravel the events because characters carry their fate with them in their features; they have no chance to meet up with it. Time is thus static, in a sense, and measures only the exhaustion of a moral action, as when there are no more gulls for the alchemists, no more dupes at the fair.

The satirist perceives evil with a one-eyed solipsism: he projects a world from the dimensionless room of his mind onto the plane of action and character without dimension. Hence all the action in a Jonson play seems to be the same. The single action of one person gulling another repeats almost indefinitely. Only the masks of the characters differ. The action of Jonson's plays, then, is determined by those masks, which in turn create the moral scene. There is no distance between the mask and the occupation of a humored character. That character does not enter a world that has its own qualities but instead creates the qualities of the world out of his own. Action and scene develop from the mask in the sense that the mask describes an "external fatality," that is, mask identifies fate as well as character. And controlling the masks of the characters is the persona of the satirist, who also has a singular obsession with the diseases he perceives. In such a world, there can be no significant change, merely cessation. In such a world, the formal unities of time and place are needed to give shape to the action, to force development and change.

The traditional Menippean satire, according to Northrop Frye, "deals less with people as such than with mental attitudes," for the satirist sees evil and folly as "diseases of the intellect."[5] As a metaphor, "disease of the intellect" suggests the combination of the physical and the intellectual that is characteristic of such comic playwrights as Aristophanes or Jonson. Aristophanes, certainly, had more specific political axes to grind and also had greater flights of imaginary fancy than Jonson (no cloud-cuckoo-land here). As playwrights they are not necessarily alike, but they do share a sense of the farcical elements of the human body and a highly critical social perception. They are intellectual playwrights not because their plays are abstract but because they combine a moral and social consciousness that is rational with the irrationality of the body. The collision of rational structures with the realities of the body is inevitably ludicrous, and both Aristophanes and Jonson exploit the collision for comic purposes. Yet they always keep us on the surface of action and character. "Diseases of the intellect" need to be perceived intellectually, as Eliot suggested of Jonson's poetry. But the rational structure tends to divide the literary and linguistic aspects of the plays from their action. In Jonson, language is not action. Humor is found not in what is said but in how it is spoken. These plays especially need to be performed, for in their foundation is a radical separation of mind and body that can be united only theatrically.

The appeal to the intellect is another aspect of Jonson's divided language. We become aware that language serves a critical function. The language in any one of Jonson's plays represents the thought and judgment of the playwright. In contrast with Shakespeare's metaphoric language, Jonson's poetry represents ideas. Instead of the preclassical *episteme* that Foucault describes, in which all texts are further commentary on a world that is already a Text, in which word and object are one, the classical *episteme* divides word and object; language, as a result, comes to "represent thought."

> One no longer attempts to uncover the great enigmatic statement that lies hidden beneath its signs; one asks how it func-

5. Northrop Frye, *Anatomy of Criticism* (Princeton, N.J.: Princeton University Press, 1957), p. 309.

tions: what representations it designates, what elements it cuts
out and removes, how it analyses and composes, what play of
substitutions enables it to accomplish its role of representation.
Commentary has yielded to *criticism*.[6]

If we were to imagine this language, for the moment, as
separate from the person who uses it, we might then see that
when the language itself has a representational and critical
function, it is both divided from and bound to the object of
representation. This language thus informs the vision of its
user. It is as though language, not the personal "vision" of the
playwright, were the source of the dystopian world. Because
Shakespeare's language is separate from the world of actuality, it provides a self-contained, mythic realm that is wholly
self-referential yet allows metaphoric thought to interpret and
attach qualities to the imaginary world of the play. The attach-
ment of words to things, conversely, virtually condemns Jonson to a dystopian attitude. He attaches meaning to the
world/word and finds it lacking in relation to the unspoken,
unrealized ideal. All that is, is present and material, for language is not free of designation. Jonson would not dally with
words, for he would not make them wanton. The source of
action is the inertia of the material world that is at once represented and criticized. In Jonson's comedy, however, delight
lies in that materiality.

The didactic purposes of Jonson's satire are related both to
specific vices and to the independent comic energy of his material world. Certain consistent vices seem to be the objects of
ridicule: moral vices like avarice or gluttony, vices of ignorance like witchcraft and alchemy. One cannot, however, presume any consistent moral philosophy that derives from the
condemnation of such vices. In Jonson, the comic intent is
identical to the moral intent. The comic intent takes whatever
is available for ridicule and consumes that material for its own
sake. It is concerned less with content than with attitude. The
specific vices that concern Jonson are occasions that allow him

6. Michel Foucault, *The Order of Things: An Archaeology of the Human Science*
(New York: Random House, Vintage Books, 1970), pp. 79–80.

to display his satiric attitude. Although there is probably no real need to condemn avarice or lust publicly, there may be a need to see how lust and avarice display themselves and how they operate. The specific vices attach themselves to the comic need for energy and excess and extremity. Ridicule is inherently critical, but the objects of criticism can be moral excuses for the pleasures of exuberance and excess. Those excesses, again, are material. The aesthetic dimension of the Jonsonian comedy, the comic energy that creates delight, comes not as much from the objects of ridicule as from the attitude of ridicule. We are thus likely to find more to laugh at in Jonson than in Shakespeare. Consider, for example, Volpone's opening speech:

> Good morning to the day; and next, my gold!
> Open the shrine that I may see my saint.
> Hail the world's soul, and mine! More glad than is
> The teeming earth to see the longed for sun
> Peep through the horns of the celestial Ram,
> Am I, to view thy splendor darkening his,
> That, lying here amongst my other hoards,
> Show'st like a flame by night, or like the day
> Struck out of chaos, when all darkness fled
> Unto the center.[7]

The speech is large. Shrine and saint, earth and sun, day and night, light and dark are not evocative, however, but almost wholly concrete and referential. Evocative language opens up a region of suggestibility between the work and the reader/audience; it ruptures the referential connection between word and object and seems to connect word and world with a "magical" authority. It calls forth but does not point at. The evocative word risks losing its identity and its communicative power by being diffused in atmosphere. The word remains, but in its evocations it becomes unlocal. Jonson's deictic words, on the other hand, are determinedly local. They stay in their place and do not move, though they point to the heav-

---

7. Ben Jonson, *Volpone*, in *Drama of the English Renaissance*, ed. M. L. Wine (New York: Random House, Modern Library, 1969), 1.1.1–10.

ens and to the center of the earth. These words represent and
point at; they carry information concretely, and though the information may be elaborate, exotic, and complex, it is also
wholly rational.

Compare, for example, Volpone's opening speech with Orsino's in *Twelfth Night*. Both are excessive in their sentiments
and ironic in their use. Both express an uncontrolled ardor
that the playwrights appear to mock. But Orsino's speech establishes a set of images that will define the concerns and
themes of the play: music, food, love. These are hardly rational "issues" but seem to evoke what Eliot called that "swarm
of inarticulate feelings." The play itself then becomes evocative in the sense that we know what it is about (music, food,
love?) but cannot concretely, empirically indicate meaning.
Volpone's speech teaches us the extent of his obsession: he
has displaced his devotions from the spiritual to the material.
Gold, identified with the sun, is more precious than light. Its
identification with the "world's soul" tells us the condition of
the world that Jonson sees: souls consumed by love of gold
and earth lit by the gleam of the profane, indeed revolving
around a gold-lit center. By extension, gold is the light of the
world, creating meaning out of chaos; it is Christ displaced to
matter. The speech that tells us the extent of Volpone's obsession declares the playwright's implicit judgment. The language operates on the principle of equivalences. Like Orsino's
speech it also declares the range and intent of the play. But the
connection between music, food, and love is intuitive—or at
least experiential—and the connection of god and gold is rational. It is a perfect and symmetrical inversion of value and
clear moral structure. The god of the world is gold; the wor-
ship of this god is evil; and the play will show us how many
times this evil can be enacted and, finally, punished. Nothing
mitigates the obsession or the inversion of value. No character
in the play provides an escape valve. Celia and Bonario are innocent, perhaps, but they do not let us escape; they belong
together, or would in a Shakespeare comedy, but Celia is already married and Bonario is helpless. The play, as many

readers have noticed, is a bestiary. As the dwarf and herma-
phrodite embody physical deformity, so each character is an
icon of moral deformity; the play is a moral zoo.

Volpone's speech is the linguistic equivalent of a mask. All
his intentions and their moral implications are exposed on the
surface of the language as he unites the world soul with his
own soul and with his gold in an orgy of materialism. There is
no personality hidden in these lines; there is only an all-
encompassing obsession that is utterly explicit. In turn, each
character wears, figuratively, a comic mask that is fixed into a
grimace, and we find the essential characteristics of each right
on the surface. Volpone's foxiness is reified and turned into an
emblem: foxiness is his grimace. In Jonson's *poesis* use and delight are combined on the surface: his images are both moral
and material. For all their autonomous delight, they also implicitly criticize. At the heart of this *poesis* is caricature.

Caricature is a source not only of laughter but also of attitudes and judgments. It is perhaps the most efficient way to
declare an attitude. As E. H. Gombrich accounts for it, caricature provides an illusion of life without the illusion of reality.

> I believe there are two conditions which account for this suc-
> cess in the illusion of life which can do without any illusion of
> reality: one is the experience of generations of artists with the
> effect of pictures, another the willingness of the public to ac-
> cept the grotesque and simplified partly because its lack of
> elaboration guarantees the absence of contradictory clues.[8]

The reductive method of eliminating "contradictory clues"
assures that the audience will see precisely what the playwright wants it to see and will make the judgments the playwright wants it to make. An audience, in turn, is comfortable
with caricature not because caricature offers an image of reality but because the audience presented with it knows exactly
what to think. It knows where it stands in relation to the action and characters. Volpone is more than a humored charac-

---

8. E. H. Gombrich, *Art and Illusion: A Study in the Psychology of Pictorial
Representation*, Bollingen Series (Princeton, N.J.: Princeton University Press,
1960), p. 336.

ter; his opening speech is more than an indication of his obsession. Both character and speech carry an attitude toward themselves that is injected by the playwright. A caricature, in short, carries its own critical attitude within it. It points to the process of selection by which the playwright directs the attention of his audience; it points to the attitude of the playwright over and above any lifelikeness in character. The necessary attention, moreover, is intellectual rather than sympathetic. Caricature seeks to create a collaboration of criticism and character in part by the conspicuous absence of realistic nuance and in part by the exaggeration of a single feature into a grotesque fixation. This exaggeration leads an audience not to character alone but to the very principles of selection. Like Brecht's *Gestus*, the caricature makes the idea of choice visible, representing complex personal and social attitudes in a simplified and perceptible image.

Caricature is the aesthetic form of exclusion, and exclusion constitutes a principle of action in Jonson's plays. The caricature collects a single moral feature totally and absolutely in itself. Like the *pharmakos*, or scapegoat figure, it takes on the poisons or diseases of society, and its exclusion allows the society to purify itself. The impulse behind the dystopian comedy, in other words, is to exclude moral evil. One of the differences between Shakespeare's humored characters and Jonson's is that Shakespeare's do not constitute the moral scheme of the play or the vision of the world: they are partial aspects of it. A character may be excluded at the end of the play, but Shakespeare's utopian structure includes as much as possible. The dystopian comedy is an "unkind" form because it establishes a world via caricature that is wholly humored, obsessed, or evil and seeks to purge, cleanse, and purify it entirely. The dystopian comedy is perhaps closer to tragedy because it conceives the world in absolutes and totalities; there is no kindness; nothing softens the harsh action of total obsession.

A normative character in a Jonsonian world would seem to make the dystopia a livable place. It would suggest to some extent that that world is possible. If Celia and Bonario were aesthetically (that is, sympathetically) available to each other, they would leave one clear and open space in the Volpone world. We would say, At least there is that. The elimination of sympathetic characters or sympathetic actions makes it impossible to find any emotional rest in the dystopia. In *Volpone* we are never led out of the world of the play. That world is a total dystopia precisely because there is no escape from a critical attitude via a norm of sympathy. There is no escape in *The Alchemist* either, where even the master of the house is complicitous. There is no societal order or potential for justice in which we might take refuge, although these constitute the primary, if unspoken, ideal, the missing dimension of a flattened world.

The dystopian comedy, on the other hand, does create another norm that serves its moral purposes. Although its vision of moral evil is singular and admits no contradictory evidence, it is still, in Jonson, a comedy. And the comedy lies not so much in the condemnation of moral evil as in the opportunity that evil provides for laughter. The dystopian comedy is an opportunistic structure; in any occasion it can, it finds the ridiculous. Morally, most of the characters in *Volpone* are reprehensible; except for Celia and Bonario, we condemn them all, the self-seeking lawyer, the merchant, and the old gentleman as well as Volpone and his parasite, Mosca. But we do not necessarily respond to the play immediately in moral terms. A character like Mosca threatens to escape the moral structure by the sheer virtuosity of his skill. As with Iago, who in performance has enormous appeal, we are in danger of liking him too much. Indeed, the ending of *Volpone*, the expulsions to the galleys and prison, is a problem only because we have come to admire the audacity of Volpone and Mosca. Audacity, in other words, has become a brand of virtue that borders on a norm of value. The value is based not on the moral structure of humors and obsessions or the clear division of good and evil but on sheer comic audacity and energy. We are vaguely disappointed that Volpone is punished, and his punishment seems arbitrary to us, particularly because we have already derived our pleasure from his actions. Jonson gives us some comic pleasure as he closes the moral barn door—a satisfying action in itself, perhaps—too late. The *dulce* of the dystopian comedy is certainly connected to the critical structure, but its own power of persuasion and its own value almost undermine its moral principles.

The undermining of the moral structure by the structure of delight is especially apparent in Mosca, who exhibits all the powers of the traditional Vice figure. In our admiration for the Vice lies the moral threat of comedy. Mosca's mobility and capacity to manipulate establish a norm. The humors in characters like Corvino or Corbaccio only make us deride them for their lack of self-consciousness. As a character appears to be more self-aware, as he is more in control of others, he takes in the audience; he comes briefly out of the world of the play to join us, then leads us back into the play, sharing with us a double consciousness of the action. We like to share the double consciousness of reality and fiction, and we like to be admitted to it by one of the play's characters who appears to be not simply a victim of the play's action but a creator of that action. Mitis and Cordatus in *Every Man out of His Humour* are somewhat abstracted instances of the double consciousness, for they mediate between the two worlds but do not actually join or control the action. Asper, on the other hand, also moves in both worlds and in disguise joins the action in the play proper. These characters give the illusion of being uncreated; they embody comic value through the illusion of control and objectivity, though their control is clearly given by the playwright himself. Just so, Mosca appears to be free of all passions; he can serve at any moment with utter duplicity, but the audacity of his lying invites the audience to admire rather than to criticize him, as we admire Richard III even as we are astonished by his audacity in winning Anne. Skill in duplicity constitutes vice, and the special skill of the Vice figure is to speak the truth so exactly that other characters fall into the trap of his deeper intent, the trap that lies under the truth. So in *Richard III* Richard can plead for charity from Anne: "You know no rules of charity / Which renders good for bad, blessings for curses" (1.2.68–69). And in *Volpone* Mosca can confess to Bonario that he has done "Base offices, in rending friends asunder, / Dividing families, betraying counsels, / Whispering false lies"(3.1.26–28). Our laughter, and the comic humor in this action (along with its potential tragedy), turns on an equal measure of horror at seeing the truth become two-sided. The skill of the Vice figure in rupturing virtue or truth generates both our alarm and our admiration. This is the double response that the comic structure as a whole can elicit: we feel both guilty admiration and moral superiority because we are equally implicated in and free of the fictional structure. The character who can speak directly to us and can be in the same room with us, acknowledging our presence as audience, speaks as the double face of the comic principle that itself is two-faced as it delights and admonishes, titillates and condemns. The principle operates with special clarity in a dystopian comedy, with its roster of moral evils combined with its intent to delight. It is a double-edged fiction in a direct line with morality plays, which explicitly divide good and evil but also delight their audiences with devilish antics and spectacular displays of the vices.

The prologue typically delivers the argument, theory, and characters of the comedy. It often asks the audience to excuse the players for the author's errors. In *Every Man out of His Humour* Jonson distorts the customary aim of the prologue by introducing Mitis and Cordatus first. When the actor for the "Prologue" finally comes out, he thanks Cordatus for doing his job for him. This illusion of improvisation is typically "comic" in that the comic form can point to itself without resorting to formality and indeed can turn formality itself to an occasion for self-display. Then, still before the play begins, another character comes out to interrupt: "Come, come, leave these fustian protestations: away, come, I cannot abide these gray-headed ceremonies." Many comedies employ such a technique of self-comment. The audience's delight in *Every Man out of His Humour* comes not simply from the farcical action of the humored characters but from the play's incorporating the audience into itself and making it part of the same world. The play confounds illusion and reality not by making them indistinguishable but by insisting on their rational unity. This effect may be ontologically unsettling to some, but for the most part it produces delight. The fictional world that acknowledges the real one lends authenticity to our reality; it validates our presence; and it gives us a double vision that includes both the fictional and the real.

Two-sided truth like Richard III's or Iago's can become tragic, but Shakespeare, not Jonson, finds it thus. In Shakespearean tragedy, the vicious characters are players, functioning at the surface, telling perfect truths, speaking to the audience, while the tragic heroes operate at both great distance and great depth. Richard III announces all his plans ahead of time, as do Iago and the witches of *Macbeth*. Iago's absolute truth about his perceptions of Desdemona ("Though I perchance am vicious in my guess / As I confess it is my nature's plague / To spy into abuses, and oft my jealousy / Shapes faults that are not" [*Othello*, 3.3.145–48]) traps Othello into self-destroying suspicions; the witches' perfect predictions ("Till Birnam wood remove to Dunsinane / . . . no man that's born of woman / Shall e'er have power upon thee" [*Macbeth*, 5.3.2–7]) lead Macbeth to false confidence in his invincibility. When the double-edged truth remains on the social plane, however, it keeps us to comedy and criticism.

The doubling in dystopian comedy extends to its value system, which is divided between the purely comic and the purely moral. On the one hand, it exploits the opportunities for ridicule or the display of daring, and the daring itself creates a norm of value. On the other hand, it seeks out justice and judgment against its obsessive characters. "Realistic" is a misnomer for this comedy. It is reductive comedy that has none of the contradictions of reality, none of the hidden motives or responsive reactions to change and circumstances, and none of the comprehensive perspective that includes shadings of human behavior. Although this comedy is realistic in contrast to the romance, perhaps, its realism is in fact a singular critical moral perspective on reality. And it is realistic in openly admitting the presence of the audience; it insists that the audience share the same theatrical space as well as the same moral sphere. But the characters or caricatures of the dystopian comedy have no interiority: they are immediate and whole and visible so that those qualities in moral nature that are customarily invisible are manifested on the surface of the human face. If the naturalistic character enhances the mystery of human nature, the humored character demystifies human nature, makes it ridiculous and therefore intelligible to the world and accessible to criticism. The corrective capacity of ridicule is not to suggest, Don't do this or you will be laughed at. It is rather to say, This is laughable. The corrective motive begins in a moral perspective that generates a contradiction between what is and what ought to be, between the picture of a diseased world and an imagined ideal of perfect health. The dialectic of that contradiction admits no qualification, no softening, no fundamental unity of virtue and vice, and no temporal or spatial dimension, for it is a dialectic of the mind. The mirror of comedy that imitates life, reflects manners, and gives truth an image does not indeed mirror a complex and contradictory reality but reflects instead the mind of its own creator, whose distortions of reality refract without dimension.

4

Wycherley's Aphorism
Delight in Dystopia

I did not care for going; but when you forbid me, you make
me, as 'twere, desire it.

The Country Wife

Margery Pinchwife's innocent truth in Wycherley's *The Country Wife* might be a lesson to all critics as well as to all jealous
husbands. As an indifferent object collects special interest
once it becomes a forbidden object, so Restoration comedies
collect special critical questions by exploiting specific moral ta-
boos. The moral issues that *The Country Wife* raises, in brief,
are specifically sexual; critics wonder whether we are meant
to approve a society founded on the free exercise of sexual indulgence, or censure it, or simply enjoy the elegant exercise of
comic form on a forbidden topic. Knowing that Horner, the
self-proclaimed eunuch, should not have his way with other
men's wives, we have a curious satisfaction that he does.
Knowing that the play ruptures the conventions of sexual morality and punishment, we still delight in it. As a genre, the
Restoration comedy habitually appeals to the special delight
in forbidden sexuality, plays indulgence against restriction,
and leaves the audience in a quandary of satisfaction. As one
critic asks: "What happens . . . if the debauched characters
seem attractive to the audience, if the satiric punishment is so
gentle or ambiguous or incomplete that it is not perceived by
the audience?"[1]

If we take Horner as emblematic of the moral and aesthetic

1. John Harwood, *Critics, Values, and Restoration Comedy* (Carbondale, Ill.:
Southern Illinois University Press, 1982), p. 99.

problem of Restoration comedy, a character admirable and reprehensible as well as enjoyable, how do we reconcile our enjoyment with our judgment? Part of the answer lies not in the playwright's intent but in the psychology of restriction and desire that Margery Pinchwife mentions. When the play exhibits the pure indulgence of sexuality in Horner's escapades, it is close to a form of wish fulfillment. At the same time, however, the play restrains and restricts that indulgence by formal decorums. I will discuss shortly the specifics of decorum in language, in the narrow society of the play's characters, in the aesthetic enclosure of the world, in the restriction of possible actions. For now, however, I am concerned only to pose a principle of delight that comes to the fore in Restoration comedy. Even in a romantic comedy, our delight in the marriage at the end of the play is heightened by the difficulties and obstacles the young couple overcome in the course of the action: the greater the obstacle, the more impossible it seems to overcome, the greater our interest in their progress and our satisfaction in their success. Our pleasure in the marriages of Olivia and Sebastian, Viola and Orsino, or even Barbara and Cusins is tied to the artificial restrictions imposed by the playwright; and it is partly our pleasure that also defines these marriages as morally good. To put it another way, our sense of aesthetic completion is at least equal to, if not greater than, a prior moral assumption that marriage is a noble estate. Restraints and difficulties serve aesthetic functions to some degree separable from a moral claim that restraint is necessary for social order. Pure wish fulfillment, in other words, is not necessarily delightful; revelry can be boring. If *Twelfth Night* consisted of nothing but songs and dances from a drunken Toby Belch, minus the impositions of Malvolio, it would quickly become tedious.

The closet scene in *The Country Wife* is a case in point. If we were to witness nothing but Horner's perfect success with his ploy, we would quickly lose interest in him. His appetite for married women might easily surfeit in our eyes so we die of boredom. In some measure, his appetite is as one-dimensional and absolute as that of any humored character.

In the closet scene, with the sudden appearance of Sir Jasper Fidget, however, that appetite is placed in a restrictive predicament. The complication and restriction of the scene make Horner's apparent success with Lady Fidget more astonishing and aesthetically wonderful because they make it all the more improbable. There is less moral onus on Horner's appetite because of the aesthetically delightful situation, or rather the moral charge in the situation is displaced into aesthetic symmetry as we watch Sir Jasper's glee when Horner and Lady Fidget are together in the "china closet."

That restrictions heighten desire and enjoyment, then, is an aesthetic principle. In drama, however, restrictions and indulgences can never be wholly formal devices. They are almost necessarily tied to further moral implications about human nature or human society. In other art forms, poetry or painting, sculpture or music, even dance, aesthetic elements can become so formal that they lead to our contemplation of a purely aesthetic object. Drama can aspire to such purity, but with human action as its material and the human being as its medium, it can never completely divorce its aesthetic devices from their human, and therefore moral, implications.

With this in mind, one can easily see why Restoration comedies present such difficulties to critics, for it is customary to look at formal, aesthetic, or delightful elements as they serve moral, ideational, or useful elements. The moral critics have complained about the Restoration comedy from its beginning. Jeremy Collier called Horner one of the "most remarkable" of the "coarse and slovenly" characters in a genre whose only purpose is "to extinguish shame and make lewdness a diversion. . . . Such licentious discourse tends to no point but to stain the imagination, to awaken folly, and to weaken the defences of virtue."[2] From this perspective, *The Country Wife* might have the same social utility as pornography and might be subject to the same moral debates. Does sexual display, in

2. Jeremy Collier, *A Short View of the Immorality and Profaneness of the English Stage*, Garland Series, *The English Stage: Attack and Defense, 1577–1730*, ed. Arthur Freeman (New York: Garland Publishing, 1972), p. 5.

other words, promote or diffuse sexual license in society? An alternative view—even of pornography—is a moral yawn; the critical version of this view is contained in L. C. Knights's famous dismissal of Restoration comedy as "trivial, gross and dull" rather than specifically immoral.[3] Just as one might complain of poor photography in erotic pictures, Knights attacks the literary qualities in Restoration comedy.

For other critics Restoration comedies are social documents whose morality simply reflects that of their elite audience in the period of the Restoration. The plays tell us as much about that society as the memoirs of Rochester or the accounts of the escapades of Charles and his mistresses. From this position, the critic neither condemns nor excuses the moral world of plays that simply represent contemporaneous society: an elite Cavalier audience that filled the galleries and formed the models for characters, an audience simply celebrating its release from Puritan oppressions.[4] This perspective offers an answer to moralistic claims against the plays that equate expression with advocacy. It also circumvents the idea that the plays are specifically satirical condemnations of the society, an idea that equates expression with criticism. Another opinion comes from Bonamy Dobrée, who finds in Wycherley's plays a "deep pessimism and a savage snarl" and in Horner specifically a "grim, nightmare figure."[5] F. W. Bateson, on the other hand, responding to L. C. Knights, finds a "serious social purpose" in Restoration comedies as a whole, a purpose that in "rationalizing . . . the sex instinct" is akin to reconciling Puritans and Royalists.[6]

For some, Restoration comedy as a genre is exempt from any absolute moral representation. "Good morality is not nec-

3. L. C. Knights, "Restoration Comedy: The Reality and the Myth," in *Restoration Drama: Modern Essays in Criticism*, ed. John Loftis (New York: Oxford University Press, 1966), p. 19.

4. See in particular Joseph Wood Krutch, *Comedy and Conscience after the Restoration* (New York: Russell and Russell, 1949), p. 45.

5. Bonamy Dobrée, *Restoration Comedy, 1660–1720* (Oxford: Clarendon Press, 1924), p. 94.

6. F. W. Bateson, "L. C. Knights and Restoration Comedy," in *Restoration Drama: Modern Essays*, p. 28.

essarily good art," says John Palmer, and a character like Horner is "immune from the censure of any other period."[7] Other critics establish systems of morality based on such value terms as *wit* or *decorum* or *freedom* or find its moral structures in "right way/wrong way" modes of behavior.[8]

The wide range of critical opinion on Restoration comedy can be explained, perhaps, by the genre's habitual forays into the morally dangerous territory of sexuality without a consistently moral attitude toward that territory. The broad range of appetites that appear in Shakespeare and Jonson is nowhere to be found in the Restoration, where the only appetite seems to be sexual. We rarely find clear censure or clear approval from the playwright. As critics and as audience we want, possibly, both to enjoy the *dulce* and to be irreproachable in that enjoyment, to indulge and to be good; and we seek a system whose terms allow both. If the content of a work seems to divorce itself from a moral scheme, then we come to value the aesthetic, formal, or artificial elements that imply some larger scheme of usefulness or morality. The *"artificielle* critics," according to John Harwood, "hold that literature is an anodyne whose moral effect is to distract the audience from its mundane concerns by immersion in a fictive world."[9] We resist the idea, that is, that any thing can be useless. Part of the difficulty in Restoration comedy is that when we apply criteria of "use," we separate aesthetics from morals. Unlike other comedies that do not disturb our values, Restoration plays send us searching for the terms of value that will allow us to enjoy their license without implying that we are licentious. *The Country Wife* puts us in a particularly difficult position if we find ourselves liking Horner or admiring his manipulation of

7. John Palmer, *The Comedy of Manners* (London: G. Bell & Sons, Ltd., 1913), pp. 288, 294. Palmer insists that critical opinion must not be confused with moral judgment.

8. Wit as the value of the good is the premise of Thomas Fujimura, *The Restoration Comedy of Wit* (Princeton, N.J.: Princeton University Press, 1952); "right-way/wrong-way" is Norman Holland's definition of the Restoration value system in *The First Modern Comedies* (Cambridge, Mass.: Harvard University Press, 1959).

9. Harwood, *Critics*, p. 52.

Pinchwife and Margery; we can admire his skill as we admire that of the Vice figure, but the play never reorders or reassembles society according to values other than Horner's, so our admiration is never superceded by moral righteousness.

On the other hand, *The Country Wife* lets us see how closely aesthetic and formal elements entwine with moral elements, or how we might derive a moral system out of aesthetic features. More specifically, if we accept restriction and indulgence as an aesthetic duality as much as a moral one, we can discover manifestations of that duality in such formal features of the play as language, scene, and character type. The containment or restriction that heightens and enhances our delight operates equally in verbal style and dramatic action. Instead of looking for justice at the end of the play, in other words, we might see how the play is aesthetically self-justified throughout. This perspective is perhaps close to that of the *artificielle* critics Harwood mentions, but it does not dismiss moral implications as irrelevant. It suggests, however, that any implied moral structure serves the purposes of delight and that we need not look for either approval or censure in the playwright's attitude or our own. *The Country Wife*, in particular, seems to balance the forbidden and the indulgent; it seems to beg for moral interpretation, yet it continually eludes moral definition.

We can, of course, see the Restoration comedies as satires that mock the very values they indulge. But if we do, we must distinguish them in both objects and means from, say, Jonson's satires. Jonson attacks the range of human temperaments that create imbalances in the moral realm of man in society. That is, he attacks moral "essences" through the notion of humors. The rhetoric is artificially constructed, to be sure, but it relies on a presumed connection between language and object. The rhetoric is instrumental, for Jonson, in attacking an imbalance in essences both in the structures of his plays and, by extension, in the structure of society. In Wycherley, the rhetoric is different. It is no accident that the plays of the period are called comedies of manners, for Wycherley and his contemporaries satirize not essences or moral "nature" but styles and their inherent attitudes. His language, moreover, is not instrumental but stylish. In Jonson, words and objects are in some sense coextensive; at the very least Jonson's language takes its qualities from the materiality of the worlds of the play. In the Restoration, objects are virtually nonexistent, as though there were no substance beneath the words at all, as though the decorums and forms of language itself were as brilliant and insubstantial as a gleam of light. If the Restoration world is satirical (and it may well be), still that satire is self-negating. Its rhetoric of highly refined decorum is a "language game" whose rules keep the indulgences of wish fulfillment within bounds. I mean to suggest that the formal elements themselves, as opposed to moral "content," constitute the tension of a moral and aesthetic unity.

Certainly it is difficult, in drama, to isolate strictly formal and aesthetic elements from moral ones. Each character, each moment of action, each speech can be perceived and defined morally, that is to say, in relation to the implicit value of each. If we look for the moment, though, at language and its qualities rather than at specific content, we get some clue about the quality of the play's world. Wycherley's language is typically aphoristic. A quick scan of *The Country Wife* offers a sample.

A quack is as fit for a pimp as a midwife for a bawd; they are still but in their way both helpers of nature.

Good wives and private soldiers should be ignorant.

'Tis my maxim, he's a fool that marries; but he's a greater that does not marry a fool.

Mistresses are like books. If you pore upon them too much, they doze you, and make you unfit for company; but if used discreetly, you are the fitter for conversation by 'em.

Women and fortune are truest still to those that trust 'em.

And any wild thing grows but the more fierce and hungry for being kept up, and more dangerous to the keeper.[10]

10. All quotations from William Wycherley's *The Country Wife* are from the text in *Six Restoration Plays*, ed. John Harold Wilson (Boston: Houghton Mifflin, Riverside Editions, 1959). The quotations are from pp. 6, 14, 15, 10, 85. Subsequent citations will be given parenthetically in the text.

The list could go on. It is easy enough to accept the ironic posture in these statements, and it would undoubtedly be a mistake to boo them off the stage as though they were indications of Restoration misogyny. I am interested in the attitude and manner of such speeches in which irony is an attitude, not a content.

These speeches continually summarize; they are conclusive; although they gain some grace from apt comparisons and witty turns, they are absolute and nonnegotiable nonetheless. They are assertive speeches, expressing no doubt, rarely qualifying themselves, often not moving the action forward. Such language does not advance into action or into sentiment or feeling. The aphorism, as its etymology suggests, "divides a territory" and puts "boundaries on the horizon." That is, the aphorism is the linguistic means of staking out a position. It is the language of the pose that defines a territory, holds all action within its bounds, and makes a spectacle of itself. The aphorism, moreover, is the linguistic version of the Restoration acting style of self-display. Taking a position down front and center, the actor makes a leg, strikes the pose, and delivers.

Our pleasure in the form of aphorism comes from the way that it holds a thought, from its formal restriction of an idea that turns the fluidity of thinking into an object. The wit of the aphorism, in turn, comes from its ability to poise natural likenesses and differences in unnatural balance. An aphorism has the form of an equation that converts natural associations, as in the first of the lines quoted above. The midwife and the bawd are morally different persons, but the same person can be both; the quack doctor and the pimp are likewise morally distinct at first glance, but the suggestion of dishonesty in a doctor makes him liable to any dishonesty and thus makes him fit to be a pimp, as though dishonesty were a mathematical constant that functions according to the distributive principle. The natural, that is, moral, distinctions between midwife and bawd, quack and pimp are equalized by the two-sided signification of "nature," on the one hand biological and on the other, moral. The biological instincts for begetting children are thus wittily turned into a "natural" morality by the careful balance of the aphoristic form. Likewise, good wives and private soldiers are formally joined by ignorance, and one cannot disprove their equation except by separating the terms from the form. But according to the criteria of wit by which it gives us pleasure, the equation is "true" because it is balanced. Similarly, the aphorism puts foolishness and marriage into a self-enclosing proportion that begins and ends with a fool taken in marriage. If one is going to be so foolish as to marry, then the only balance for that action is to marry a fool (in another sense of the word—one who is ignorant), but the result is a marriage of two fools.

The status of the aphorism is both absolute and precarious. It cannot be disproved or even argued except by putting its assertion into some other form, for example, discourse, at which point it loses its identity and its truth. The aphorisms are true only in their form; in the fluidity of discourse or in the flux of real experience, they quickly become nonsense; but their satisfaction comes from the temporary stillness and perfect balance. The wit of the aphorism often comes from making unlikely associations as assertions of truth, as in the following example. Sir Jasper Fidget has just spoken of woman as "that sweet, soft, gentle, tame, noble creature, woman, made for man's companion." Horner replies: "So is that soft, gentle, tame and more noble creature a spaniel, and has all their tricks; can fawn, lie down, suffer beating, and fawn the more; barks at your friends when they come to see you, makes your bed hard, gives you fleas, and the mange sometimes. And all the difference is, the spaniel's the more faithful animal, and fawns but upon one master" (p. 27). This speech is not an aphorism, but it is presented as declarative truth. I am suggesting how the form of the language creates the quality of both the characters we perceive and the world of the play. Like a maxim, *The Country Wife* has very little of the geniality of discussion.

In an essay on La Rochefoucauld, Roland Barthes describes

the difference between discourse and maxim in precisely the terms of quality that I am suggesting for the rhetoric of the Restoration. In discourse, he said, there is

> a certain fragility, a certain discursive caution, a language more delicate, more open to kindliness, as if, conversely, the maxim could only be mean—as if the closure of the maxim were also a closing of the heart. . . .
>
> . . . a normal sentence, a *spoken* sentence always tends to dissolve its parts into each other, to equalize the flux of thought; it progresses, in short, according to an apparently unorganized process; in the maxim, the converse is the case; the maxim is a general unit composed of particular units; the skeleton—and bones are hard things—is more than apparent: spectacular.[11]

I am not suggesting that *The Country Wife* is one large sententious maxim but that the world of the play is "hard" like the maxim, pared down to essentials, closed off from the fluctuation of change. In other words, one element of the play that gives us the sense of a heartless world is the aphoristic form of its language. Characters take poses in their speeches and offer proofs of their positions. They do not invite any sympathy from the audience, though the audience may try to give sympathy. Like the maxim, the play closes itself off from feeling by its rational construction of language. It never hesitates or qualifies its presentation. The language is "spectacular" in being more like written speech than spoken thought; it has the conclusiveness and the fixation that customarily belong to writing, not talking.

The brutality that some critics have seen in this world might well be attributed to the hardness of the form of the play itself, not to some deep cynicism or dark satirical purpose that is hidden from view. Brutality comes not simply from amoral or immoral actions or from moral content alone but from the fixture of positions, an absence of the expectation of or desire for change. And the audience is complicitous, neither expecting nor wanting Horner to change; we want and

11. Roland Barthes, "La Rochefoucauld," in *New Critical Essays*, trans. Richard Howard (New York: Hill and Wang, 1980), pp. 4–5.

applaud the perpetuation of his seeming/being ploy, though I doubt we would necessarily complain if he were somehow punished, for we have no emotional stake in Horner, or in Pinchwife, or in the Fidgets. We have a stake in the wittiness of the play—the pleasure of form—not in the characters. The particular dystopia of this play, then, does not come from represented world or from the satirical vision of the playwright, as it did in Jonson, although if we imagined this world as real, we would certainly see a dystopian place. This dystopia comes from the hardness of the language itself, from the sense of a purely artificial moral world created out of a form of writing. The dystopias of Wycherley and Shaw share a sense that the world of the play emerges from words, but where Shaw's words are discursive and therefore aimed at utilitarian effectiveness, Wycherley's words fix themselves to the pure formalism of the maxim. The *dulce* element of pure formality helps create an unkind world made out of the brutality of words in mathematical shapes. Shaw's language aims at persuasion; Wycherley's language aims at self-enclosed artifice with no apparent desire to persuade.

From this perspective, we can imagine that wit is a value not simply for the characters in the play but for the play itself. The wit of the aphorism creates value in the artifact as an object. As critics, we often want to get away from the surface to plumb the depths of intention and implication, but this Restoration comedy continually insists on its surfaces and on its spectacle, for even its language is spectacular. The world of the play is dystopian because of its hardness. It refuses to embrace us with the "kindliness" of discourse; morally, it is not a world that "ought" to be, but its artifice suggests that it can be no other way.

The hardness of the world is evident in the wit that perceives a perfect inversion or system of opposites. Horner, for example, says, "Your arrantest cheat is your trustee or executor, your jealous man, the greatest cuckold, your churchman the greatest atheist, and your noisy pert rogue of a wit, the greatest fop, dullest ass, and worst company" (p. 12). We value such a speech only partly for its moral content. We appreciate the extremity and opposition of a moral perception and an artificial formulation. The speech excludes an enormous amount of detail, perhaps, but thus has the essence of a caricature that is minimal but comprehensive. Like the aphorism, it justifies itself, and its very self-completion is satisfying. For some, the speech indicates Horner's cynicism, which it may well show, but it is also an elegant assertion whose value lies in its elegance. It is language that makes a spectacle of itself, to paraphrase Barthes, and that spectacle is inversion. The motive of such inversion is less to arrive at a truth than to display extremities.

The wits of the Restoration world see ironically, not because irony is true but because it is elegant. The oppositions in the speech above suggest the paradoxical irony that Shavian characters see in the world: "My greatest friend is my bravest enemy," says Undershaft. But where Shaw uses his paradoxes to reach toward a larger, almost metaphysical, perception, Wycherley uses his to reach toward the perfection of an artifact, so that we think of Shaw at an extreme of *utile* and of Wycherley at an extreme of *dulce*. Shaw has lessons to teach through pleasurable means; Wycherley would give us simply lessons in pleasure. The world of Wycherley's play is not necessarily a pleasant one: as a representation it resists our liking, our sympathy, and our own kindliness because of its elegant enclosure. We cannot enter its display, nor does it join with us.

The sense of restriction in the scene of *The Country Wife* is only partially dependent on the narrowness of the society the play portrays, a society consisting of young gallants, a sparkish fop, a jealous husband and his wife, ladies of the town, an all-important maid, and a doctor. For the most part this cast belongs to a single social stratum that implies no hierarchical values like those we find in Shakespeare. It may well be true that the play mirrors the elite and narrow audience of the Restoration period and employs recognizable types for its social images. Beyond its immediate imitation or reflection of that society, however, its compression of value tightly encloses its world. One can give that value any one of a number of names, wit or success, style or gallantry, but none has much to do with conventional features of moral value. Hence the difficulty in reconciling the comic delight of the play with any external system of value. The play is compressed by the singleness of its concern. Its inverted world is less than significative in social terms, dangerous in moral ones because it fixates on sexuality as the center of society. Not the class system itself but the domination of all relations and actions by sexuality narrows the world. In some sense, sexuality is the scene of the play even though we move from Horner's lodgings to Pinchwife's house to the New Exchange. The particulars of place are not much more than occasions for variations on sexual gambit. The scene dominates characters and action in such a way that it seems to mirror not an external society but a core of sexual instinct. The range of possible actions is thus narrowed to permutations of that single issue.

In precise terms, Harcourt and Alithea are exceptions because marriage is their promised end. But their marriage is not so much distinct from the scene of sexuality as it is distant from the center. As characters, they both belong in the Restoration scene as opposed, say, to a romantic or sentimental one; and as agents of dramatic structure they provide a moral limit to the world that keeps the Horner excess from spilling over. From the first we see Harcourt as a realist, not a dewy-eyed romantic; he is clearly a member of the wit world in good standing. When he says, "Mistresses are like books," he distinguishes his own sense of balance and proportion in regard to women from Horner's excessive cynicism.

> HORNER: Wine gives you joy; love, grief and tortures, besides the chirurgeon's. Wine makes us witty; love, only sots. Wine makes us sleep; love breaks it.
> DORILANT: By the world, he has reason, Harcourt.
> HORNER: Wine makes—
> DORILANT: Ay, wine makes us—makes us princes; love makes us beggars, poor rogues, egad—and wine—
> HORNER: So, there's one converted.—No, no, love and wine, oil and vinegar.
> HARCOURT: I grant it; love will still be uppermost.
>
> (p. 11)

However briefly, we are being prepared to value Harcourt as a lover. Granting all the contradictions of women and wine

(wine that makes Dorilant stumble and Horner hesitate), love will still be uppermost. Harcourt seems to understand both proportion and love, and we are prepared to believe that he is capable of love beyond lust. We match him with Alithea, the other reasonable creature in the play, who also appears to have a sense of balance and proportion, who is not naive yet takes "the innocent liberty of the town," who values marriage, honor, and commitment.

In a Shakespearean play, Harcourt and Alithea would probably stand at the center of the social and moral order; they would be the heart of the play around which other characters would gather in concentric rings. The romance requires just such a center of value as it replicates an idea of order based on ideal love. At least one critic asserts that Harcourt and Alithea do stand "at the center of the play"; another believes that they at least hint at "true standards of judgement."[12] These assessments suggest how eagerly we seek characters who demonstrate a central value on which all others depend and how well a romance pair suits the needs of such centrality. Rosalind and Orlando are central in the world of *As You Like It* and in some measure represent a standard of judgment. But *The Country Wife* does not revolve around Harcourt and Alithea. One critic has suggested they are present for "necessary fullness and variety,"[13] and this, I think, is somewhat closer to the point. Their romance is derivative; they set limits on Horner's world in the suggestion of a sound marriage, but they establish no ideal in the play. Their marriage does not represent a conversion of the society out of its dystopia, for the dance at the end is a dance of cuckolds, not of happy couples.

As a dramatic function, the pairing of Harcourt and Alithea

12. Anne Righter and Kenneth Muir, respectively, quoted in Robert D. Hume, *The Development of English Drama in the Late Seventeenth Century* (Oxford: Clarendon Press, 1976), p. 101.
13. Ibid. Hume himself contradicts the positions of Righter and Muir: "If Harcourt and Alithea are supposed to represent a high moral norm in the play and make us view Horner with disapprobation, then Wycherley made a mess of things. For in practice one is benevolently indifferent to the couple during the play and scarcely remembers them in it afterwards."

propitiates some of our moral objections to the rest of the play. To some extent it diffuses the unrelenting comic energy of the sex farce with sentiment. As critics we perhaps submit to the value of the pairing out of habit and might like to enlarge its significance as the last vestige of romance in a corrupt world, but the comic interest and dramatic energy are elsewhere. The inevitability of Harcourt and Alithea's marriage allows us to enjoy the unexpected turns of Horner's ploy all the more because they are safely contained. And the constraint of Harcourt and Alithea's romance allows us to indulge our pleasure in Horner and his ladies not because that romance is central but because it is peripheral. Harcourt and Alithea offer no renewal of the world, nor is their marriage a ritual celebration of hope that a utopian romantic comedy might offer. They are both realists in this world. The play, however, offers at least one hint of the sentimental dramas to come. "Can there be a greater cheat or wrong done to a man than to give him your person without your heart?" (p. 47), asks Lucy, Alithea's maid. In this small indictment of the Horner-value in the play we can hear the whisper of a sentimental antidote for the sexual scene. The heart is at the core of sentimental sensibilities and develops as a moral force in the later sentimental comedies. Here Lucy offers the "heart" as a value that supersedes Alithea's honorable intent toward Sparkish, her unlovable fiancé. Already it appears as a self-justified moral value, as a higher source of morality than honor. In a Shakespearean romance, for example, it is unnecessary to appeal to the heart as an antidote to a society corrupted by sexuality and acquisitive motives, for Shakespeare's world is not dialectically divided in those terms. The dystopia of a society founded on sexuality, however, calls out for its opposite, for this world has severed the connection between sexual instinct and feeling and, however incidentally, seeks a reconciliation. In a character like Horner, wit and its powers of rational perception and judgment are fully in service to instinct, and the rupture between sexual instinct and feeling is the basis of the satirical strain of the play. I do not mean to suggest that the play is in any way sentimental or that its aim is to reconcile sexual instinct and feeling. But the moral strain against the form is such that the world of the play invites a sentimental deflation. There are strains of both farce and satire in *The Country Wife*. Pinchwife, Jasper Fidget and his wife, Lady Squeamish, Sparkish, Margery are all set up for us as objects of ridicule, examples of errors, hypocrisy, excess, blindness. We know immediately what their various errors are and how those errors led them to their comic predicaments. Pinchwife is living proof that overzealous protection of one's wife causes and spurs the wife's desire. In an elegant extension of the principle, Pinchwife delivers not only a love letter from his wife to her lover but his wife herself as well. At the other extreme, Sir Jasper Fidget delivers lover to wife out of overzealous interest in business. Lady Fidget and Squeamish, if not punished for their hypocrisy, are at least stuck with it, being forced to keep their knowledge a secret. Like Jonsonian caricatures, these characters typify their obsessions. They are well within the tradition of comic types who exhibit the single dimension of a moral point.

Depending on one's point of view, the play satirizes lust, rigidity, foppish excess, sexual repression, innocence, false seeming, witlessness: the possibilities are extensive. But what sort of errors are these? Do character types and obsessions contain the moral premises of the playwright or do they simply create the foundation for comic possibilities? Obviously there is an overlap between moral premises and comic possibilities, but we seem to keep asking for the playwright's intent beneath the comic uses of moral materials. Rigidity, for example, is a moral problem. It is made to be broken as much as husbands are made to be cuckolds. The dramatic principle is not so much that rigidity or marriage is wrong as that each one carries in it the principle of opposition that makes extreme reversals both necessary and probable.

Sometimes a play offers its own judgment by using the principle of reversal as evidence of retribution, as when Volpone and Mosca are sent off to prison and the galleys by the Avocatori. Law comes in from the outside to deliver their fate; characters unmask; or disguises are discarded. In *The Country*

Wife, however, there is no such imposition of justice, and Horner's disguise slips but is not removed. In another play we might expect that Margery would never reach Horner's closet, or that Pinchwife at some point would become aware of his moral error, or that the wives would be publicly ostracized, or that Horner would be banished. But here there is no holding back from the deed, no public renunciation or revelation. Pinchwife discovers that he has mistakenly delivered his wife to her lover, but he never recognizes that his own moral error made him her purveyor. He chooses further self-deception, as Sir Jasper continues his, as Horner chooses continued public deception for private gains. The play teeters on the edge of revelation but never falls over. It is saved by the complicity of silence among its characters, although Margery would like to reveal all. Since the characters never unmask, since they insist on continuing both public and private deceptions, the play does not leave the world of its artifice; it never emerges from itself but rather turns back on itself. The audience can feel slightly cheated of a conclusion, can feel perhaps the dark implications of continuing deceptions, but the play resists the audience until its epilogue. Until then, it maintains the obdurate surfaces of an artifact seen at a distance. It refuses to acknowledge itself as a fictional deception except in the occasional aside because it is so wholly committed to self-display.

The motive of self-display brings us back to the motives of wit. True wit in characters partly manifests itself in the presentation of an idea as an object rather than as a revelation of the self. Wit is not a communication; it allows no interaction. It exists outside the human being or is like a game that characters play, separate from their persons. Wit is manufactured and set out for all to see. Sparkish is not a wit in part because he continually proclaims himself in his speech. His wish to be accepted, his desire for fellowship, his eagerness to join are all too apparent. Unlike Horner or Harcourt or Dorilant, he cannot divorce himself from his speech and make his speech an object; we see too much of him when he talks, and he thus turns himself into an object for ridicule. Pinchwife, too, reveals too much of himself and his single concern. And Margery reveals too much earnest innocence. The wits separate themselves from what they say and operate at a distance. This gives them less "character" in one way but more power in another. The unwitty characters too often mean what they say, and thus are more available as objects of ridicule. Wit makes characters invulnerable to attack; it protects and contains them. But wit is also the aesthetic element that makes almost any comedy of manners appear shallow; it allows no penetration into character. At the same time, however, because it is a source of delight, it becomes a value in itself.

Wit both helps to make comedy of manners impenetrable and gives it a value. It thus creates an aesthetic surface that resists a sentimental conclusion, for it makes no appeal to the heart. The final summary of the lesson of *The Country Wife* is a formal one, a statement of principle:

> LUCY: And any wild thing grows but the more fierce and hungry for being kept up, and more dangerous to the keeper.
> ALITHEA: There's doctrine for all husbands, Mr. Harcourt.
> HARCOURT: I edify, madam, so much, that I am impatient till I am one.
> DORILANT: And I edify so much by example, I will never be one.
> SPARKISH: And because I will not disparage my parts, I'll ne'er be one.
> HORNER: And I, alas! can't be one.
> PINCHWIFE: But I must be one—against my will to a country wife, with a country murrain to me!
> MARGERY: (*Aside*) And I must be a country wife still too, I find; for I can't, like a city one, be rid of my musty husband, and do what I list.
>
> (p. 85)

This round of affirmations is more explicitly conclusive than many comic endings. The lesson is clear and all characters acknowledge their relation to it. Perhaps it jars with our knowledge that Horner will continue his deception and that the Pinchwifes will continue a marriage of tension, but it is a clear and formal completion of the doctrine of repression. Its very formality creates the structure of containment that has allowed us to enjoy the indulgence of Horner's exploits. This formal completion asserts an aesthetic value that may be at odds with moral implications, or at least with our feeling about how the world ought to be. That feeling says we ought not to approve of Horner's deception or, further, that the gulf between dissembling and truth ought to be bridged. But aesthetically we admire Horner. The play continually tosses the audience between moral disapproval and astonished admiration, attempting to convert our disapproval by its assertive audacity. It dares the audience to take it seriously but repels all attempts to do so. Like the hard surface of a mirror, it appears to reflect society but is finally only a surface.

This illusion requires a means of convincing the audience or converting it to the truth of the illusion. The character who aids and abets the illusion for the audience, as well as for Horner, is Quack. In narrative terms, he is present simply to spread the rumor of Horner's impotence and to confirm it to the husbands at the end of the play. But for the audience he serves a further function. The doctor helps to assuage our incredulity. He makes Horner's audacity plausible even as he subdues any astonishment at it.[14] The doctor takes the audacity of the ploy as preposterous, "as ridiculous as if we operators in physic should put forth bills to disparage our medicaments, with hopes to gain customers" (p. 7). Finally, though, he is convinced. The doctor verifies for himself, from behind the screen, the efficacy of the ploy, and his own amazement reduces our critical distance, helping to convert us. We agree with him that men are not what they seem and that disguise is the most effective premise for action. We comply with what our moral sense tells us ought not to be true, for the very extremity of the premise is astonishing: the saddest eunuch is

14. Harwood, *Critics*, p. 104. Harwood's account of Quack's function is similar to mine: "What *The Country Wife* provides for the doctor and the audience, which may be as skeptical as the doctor about Horner's experiment, is a test of a new procedure, a new chemistry, for procuring mistresses. Horner has become the doctor, the chemist of human relations, and his alembic is the social world reflected in Sir Jasper and his women, Pinchwife and Sparkish. . . . The 'education' of the doctor in the ways of the world may mime the kind of education that the comedy offers to its audience."

the greatest rogue. The collapse of seeming and being into one image is both morally offensive and formally wonderful. And because no justice is finally imposed on Horner, because he will continue the deception, there seems no end to the collapse; the game will continue, breaking all the rules of the real world.

The humor of the play depends heavily on our sense of those rules. We must know that deception, hypocrisy, rampant lust are essentially antisocial or we will not laugh at their rupture. But the play itself will not acknowledge its attitude toward the rules, and we laugh at the doubling of standards as we laugh in the famous china closet scene, in which there is no indication that Horner and Lady Fidget are discussing anything but the sale of china. Horner continually invites retribution, but his skill and the complicity of the doctor repulse the wheels of justice and revelation.

The formal containment of sexual indulgences in *The Country Wife* leaves us with the principle of Margery's statement quoted in the epigraph of this chapter. With a slight alteration, we would say, "I did not care for morality, but when you forbid it, you make me, as 'twere, desire it." For this play constantly provokes our moral sensibilities while it insists that we enjoy its indulgences. Unless we insist on a definitive moral and ethical posture, the play stays alive in the contradiction of desire and forbidden territory, suggesting that the pleasure of form and aesthetic artifice can make even a dystopian world a delight.

5

Cumberland and Steele's Aphorism
Use in Utopia

> If pleasure be worth purchasing, how great a pleasure is it
> to him who has a true taste of life to ease an aching heart, to
> see the human countenance lighted up into smiles of joy on
> the receipt of a bit of ore which is superfluous and otherwise
> useless in a man's own pocket? What could a man do better
> with his cash?
>
> The Conscious Lovers

If ever a comedy excited little or no moral controversy, it is
Steele's play *The Conscious Lovers*. Here is the union of precept
and example, a play as certain of its values and as explicit in
their expression as a play can be without leaving the realm of
drama. Steele's own stated purpose for writing the drama was
to set an example for the young gallants of the eighteenth-
century audience. Specifically, he wrote a scene in which Bevil's friend, Myrtle, wrongfully accuses him of having designs
on Myrtle's beloved, Lucinda; Bevil resists the impulse to defend his honor, refuses to come to a duel, and keeps his
friendship with Myrtle. Steele said of this scene: "This Example would have been of great Service; for since we see young
Men are hardly able to forbear Imitation of Fopperies on the
Stage, from a Desire of Praise, how warmly would they pur-
sue true Gallantries, when accompanied with the Beauties
with which a Poet represents them, when he has a Mind to
make them amiable?"[1]

---

1. Richard Steele, *The Theatre, 1720*, ed. John Loftis (Oxford: Clarendon
Press, 1962), p. 83. As Loftis points out, the play was not produced until two
years after this "half-sheet" biweekly was written, but it must have been by
then "nearly completed" (p. ix). On the same topic, the dangers of the audience imitating what it sees on stage, see also *The Spectator*, no. 65.

One cannot imagine any of the typical attacks on comedy brought against such a play: far from "speaking smuttily" (Jeremy Collier's complaint against the Restoration comedies), the men and women of sentiment express only the noblest ideals and the most honest feelings; no excess of humors or obsessions moves the characters; no satire is directed against social institutions; marriage is a sacred estate, not a repressive confinement; and no Vice figure appears to mock the righteous. The audience at such a play should emerge edified and filled with examples of those positive virtues that will best govern their lives.

The call for generosity in the speech quoted in the epigraph of this chapter might well have come from a Protestant pulpit before the passing of a collection plate; in fact, it comes from Bevil Junior of *The Conscious Lovers* during a conversation on the theoretical question whether a man "ever does any extraordinary kindness or service for a woman but for his own sake" (2.2.48–50).[2] The question is apt, for Bevil has recently rescued his questioner, Indiana, from a menacing lawyer; seen her safely to England; supported her "in the condition of a woman of quality" (2.2.44); and sent along two hundred fifty pounds for a "set of dressing plate." Indiana may well wonder at Bevil's motives, may well question whether Bevil expects a return. But Bevil's motives are pure, if not wholly disinterested, and his generosity is sincere. In his respect for womanhood, Bevil is setting yet another example for an audience of gallants.

What strikes us now about Bevil's speech is its excess and insincerity: how, we ask, is it possible not only to feel such generosity but also to speak it in such an unconvincing style? In fact, in the very issue of sincerity the eighteenth-century sentimental comedy draws attention to itself.

The content and quality of sentimental comedy has been well documented. The genealogy of the "man of feeling" has

2. All quotations from Richard Steele's *The Conscious Lovers* and Richard Cumberland's *The West Indian* are taken from *Plays of the Restoration and Eighteenth Century*, ed. Dougald MacMillan and Howard Jones (New York: Henry Holt, 1931). Subsequent citations will be given parenthetically in the text.

been traced by R. S. Crane through the sermons and essays of the Anglican divines of the latitudinarian tradition.[3] The principles Crane enumerates are both "ethical and psychological"; they suggest that the ethical ideals of the eighteenth century are not abstractions but immediate and concrete psychological realities. The foundation of the tradition is benevolence: from the example of God's feeling, men and women act benevolently toward one another. Such an attitude is clearly evident in Bevil's concern not only for the destitute Indiana but also for his friend Myrtle and for his own father as well.

Language in *The Conscious Lovers*, moreover, is something like that of a sermon. Richard Cumberland particularly criticized the "sickly sentimental cast" of the dialogue in this play and complained that "sentiment is always to be had, when incident cannot be so conveniently invented, or character supported."[4] But even with less sentiment and a broader range of character types, Cumberland's play *The West Indian* exhibits similar qualities.

The sense of sermonizing is somewhat misleading, I think, insofar as it suggests preaching directly to an audience. The preaching, if it is that, comes indirectly through the agency of character. The sermonic quality is in the "consciousness" of a character like Bevil, aware of both his own feelings and the ideal of behavior to which he submits. What seems impossible now is any such harmonious coalescence of feelings and ideal behavior. Even though such a union is highly unlikely, it tells us something about the sentimental character as a dramatic artifice. We object, legitimately, to a young man's so innocently devoting his pocketbook to a young, beautiful Indiana and to his speaking, furthermore, so eloquently, if excessively, about the precept of generosity. But if we look past the likelihood to the implicit notion of dramatic character, then we see that for a character like Bevil Junior personal emotions are

3. R. S. Crane, "Suggestions toward a Genealogy of the 'Man of Feeling,'" in *The Idea of the Humanities*, vol. 1 (Chicago: University of Chicago Press, 1967), pp. 188–213.
4. Richard Cumberland, "Critique on *The Conscious Lovers*," in Richard Steele, *Comedy of the Conscious Lovers* (London: C. Cook, n.d.), p. xiv.

identical to larger ethical ideals. There is thus little distinction between the action of such a character and his consciousness of the *principle* of action. Speech is a gesture of both that principle and its cooperative emotions, which together create the sentimental character. The creation of this unity brings us again to the notion of sincerity. What we now may dismiss as insincere, because it seems impossible, is in fact "sincerity," inasmuch as *sincerity* means "the same in actual character as in outward appearance."

As awkward as Bevil's speech to Indiana may seem, we are meant to believe that Bevil both feels and means what he says. It may even be that we feel the awkwardness of the speech because we believe it. Our more modern sense of sincerity is that we should say less than we feel: a silent dramatic character for us is often the most apparently sincere; insofar as that character has lost the language that matches feelings, he or she says nothing. In the eighteenth century, however, language could still take shape around emotion, and character stood at the nexus. Passions were not anathema to the sentimental character but were considered an element of his humanity. To the sentimental character the unity of those inward emotions with the outward is crucial. This unity lies in the sincerity that in turn can define for us the way that the rhetoric of the sentimental play works. That the sentimental comedy lacks verisimilitude has long been understood. But we have ignored the relation between sincerity and the usefulness of both the sentimental character (who exemplifies precepts) and the sentimental form itself as it attempts to participate in the real world as a model of behavior.

What we might call the rhetoric of sincerity relies on the assumption that actuality coincides with appearance, that the hidden inner realm is the same as its expression. Sincerity is the basis of our trust that unlike poor Duncan we can indeed "find the mind's construction in the face." We might extend this principle into a sense that the sentimental drama also proffers sincerity to its audience. The sentimental play, that is, is as trustworthy as its characters: it appears as a realistic world in which there is no apparent dissembling by artifice and play. We do not have to guess whether the play is telling us to emulate or avoid its examples. It is a world "like ours," apparently without the trappings of artifice and self-display. It is thus the polar opposite of the world of wit, in which the greatest values are aesthetic and in which we delight in performance. In the rhetoric of sincerity there is no pretense, no acting, no conscious performance for an audience because that rhetoric is meant to be exemplary. The world is on display not for its own sake but for the sake of the interior truth. In the sentimental utopia we find that the interior values are identical to the external social and mercantile values. In the economy of the sentimental world, the value of the aphorism is not in its style but in its content: language, that is, loses its independence from meaning and is bound to assertions of the truth that is hidden, on the one hand, in the inner recesses of human emotions and projected, on the other, to the realm of divine Providence.

There is an implicit equation of inner and outer value in Bevil's speech to Indiana. The terms of the equation are pleasure and purchase; the aching heart and smiles of joy; the superfluous bit of ore and the joy of the giver. These terms suggest a sentimental economy in which the exterior medium of exchange, money, is scarcely distinguishable from the interior medium of exchange, the heart. Generosity with that bit of superfluous ore is the external show of an interior exchange: the giving and receiving in the social sphere of the heart, of benevolence, and ultimately of divinity. Money, as Bevil Junior suggests, can purchase pleasure insofar as it is able to transform heartache into a smile of joy. Cash is the superfluous dross whose significance lies hidden in the human heart. It stands on the plane of social exchange and replicates the motions of the heart on the surfaces of society. And what makes this unity possible is the sincerity of the giver.

The unity of cash and character, wealth and worth is one of the distinctions of sentimentality. In the comedies of moral humors wealth usually signals avarice or provides—in *Volpone*, for example—an occasion for greed and cunning. Linked to the tradition of morality plays and such characters as Worldly-Lyking or Goods, wealth is virtually a sign of corruption in society or of moral error in human nature. The genuine devaluation of material fortune, however, in a play like *The Merchant of Venice*, leads to a discovery of moral worth. Bassanio chooses the lead casket over the gold and silver ones and thereby gains a true fortune in Portia. The sentimental comedy, conversely, devalues money as a "superfluous bit of ore" and at the same time exalts it as evidence of a good and magnanimous spirit. But this spirit of the interior is bound to the evidence of the exterior not by speech but by sincerity. The connection between language and meaning, therefore, is removed from the surfaces of words to the invisible and ineffable reaches of the human heart. This removal implies, on the one hand, that language has no value other than its "sincerity factor" and, on the other, that language testifies to the consciousness of sincerity.

Bevil Junior's speech is a statement of principle that in turn is a gesture of character. He is indeed a walking sermon, but that sermon is sensible to human emotion. The "man of feeling" is not divided by reason and emotion; his conscious refinement of feelings, his awareness of their function, and his determination to do the right thing unite his mind and heart and seem to satisfy both ethical principles and personal desires. Such a unity is present in the habitual self-explanation of sentimental characters. The interiority of feeling is brought to the level of conscious ethical principles. More important, those ethical principles suggest an ideal society based on personal ethics and good fellow feeling. There is no conflict between the individual and society. We are in a hypothetical world based almost entirely on character. And because there is virtually no friction between the individual and the social order, we find a utopia. Character, feeling, action, and ethical principles are so closely connected that there is no dialectical level with which to open this world to criticism.

Events in the sentimental comedies are constructed primarily to display feelings and to confirm the ethical principles of feelings in characters. Dramatic action thus serves to demonstrate faith, good will, forbearance, or honesty, so the plot becomes merely the occasion for the appearance of virtues. Although the characters are generally very simple, the plots are notoriously complex. A good example of the convoluted sentimental plot is that of *The West Indian*. Since this play is less familiar than *The Conscious Lovers*, an account of the plot may be helpful.

Young Belcour (Good Heart) is returning to England from Jamaica, where he was raised by his mother and grandfather. He is heir to his grandfather's estate, though his grandfather knew him only as a foundling. Belcour's mother, secretly married to her father's clerk Stockwell, had kept her son's identity a secret from her father, fearing his anger and retribution for her marriage. Stockwell himself has lived in England, where he has become a successful merchant and member of Parliament. Belcour and Stockwell have been corresponding, but Stockwell has never revealed the secret of Belcour's birth. Stockwell has decided to test his son's character before revealing himself as his father.

Also in London are a Captain Dudley, his son Charles, and his daughter Louisa. The impoverished captain has come to seek the financial aid of his sister-in-law, Lady Rusport, whose step-daughter Charlotte is in love with young Charles Dudley. Lady Rusport is being courted by an Irish soldier of fortune, Major O'Flaherty. Some fairly complicated financial and romantic interests intertwine the two groups. Lady Rusport refuses Captain Dudley's appeal, much to the disappointment of Charlotte, who offers her jewels to Stockwell as security for a loan for the captain and his family. Belcour, in the meantime, has glimpsed Louisa Dudley in the street and has followed her to her lodgings, which are run by the down-and-out Fulmers. Mrs. Fulmer, out to make a profit whenever she can, tells Belcour that Louisa is the mistress of Charles (her brother, in fact) and that she could help out his interest in Louisa with some baubles to purchase favors. In the meantime, Belcour has also heard the plight of Captain Dudley and spontaneously offers him the mere two hundred pounds that Dudley needs to join the regiment in Senegambia. Belcour is then entrusted with Charlotte's jewels by Stockwell, who means to make her a loan without that security; but *en route* to Charlotte Belcour succumbs to temptation and delivers the jewels to Mrs. Fulmer in hopes of gaining access to Louisa.

Major O'Flaherty, in the meantime, has met Captain Dudley and has also become sympathetic to his plight. When he learns of Lady Rusport's pitiless, hard heart, the major renounces her immediately. Charlotte is attempting to make Charles Dudley declare his love for her, but without success. Belcour enters shortly to confess that he disposed of the jewels, finds Louisa in the company of Charlotte, and claims that Louisa has the jewels. The insult to his sister's honor forces Charles to disparage Belcour's honor, at which point Belcour challenges him to a duel.

Lady Rusport then meets a lawyer who reports the existence of a new will of her father's, one that gives the entire estate to Captain Dudley. They plot to suppress this new will but are overheard by Major O'Flaherty. As the threads of the plot are wound to a climax at the scene of the duel, the Fulmers are brought to confess, O'Flaherty reveals the plot of the will, Stockwell reveals himself as Belcour's father, Charlotte and Charles finally declare their love, Belcour apologizes to Louisa, and Belcour and Louisa are betrothed. The captain is saved from his certainly fatal trip to Senegambia, and Lady Rusport departs in disgrace.

This is a far more complicated plot than that of *The Conscious Lovers*, in which all the efforts are directed toward getting four lovers properly paired in spite of parental plans. The villains in *The West Indian* are more clearly defined as villains. Cimberton, Lucinda's suitor, comes closest to villainy in *The Conscious Lovers* only because his interest in Lucinda is based on economic advantage and a secret admiration for the heave of her bosom. He provides a nominal obstacle to the union of Lucinda and Myrtle but serves primarily as a foil and a distraction from the potential rivalry between Bevil Junior and Myrtle. Cimberton, in other words, does not take an active role in villainy whereas both the Fulmers and Lady Rusport are conscious villains, and both provide some humor in their play. The Fulmers, at least, invite a comparison to the comic husband and wife team that stems from Noah and his wife in the morality plays. They fuss and feud in typical style. More important, perhaps, they are moral outsiders in the society: they are Catholic, economically unsuccessful (perhaps, the play suggests, because they are Catholics), not lawfully wedded, scheming, and greedy.

No characters like the Fulmers and Lady Rusport appear in *The Conscious Lovers*. Tom and Phyllis are servants with rustic names, but even they fully share the sensibility of the conscious world. Their exchanges are just slightly rougher versions of the exchanges of Bevil Junior and Indiana, Myrtle and Lucinda, characters with middle-class sensibilities. Cumberland, in fact, objected to one exchange between Tom and Phyllis because of Steele's failure to maintain a class distinction: "I wish Tom had not alluded to Pyramus and Thisbe; the simile would not naturally occur to a man in his sphere."[5] He objects, that is, on the grounds of verisimilitude: servants and classical references do not mix.

For all their genuine differences, there are similarities between *The West Indian* and *The Conscious Lovers* that typify the sentimental structure and help reveal the sentimental myth. In this structure background is crucial: events that occurred before the play's action and are reported by one of the characters serve, in general, as moral justification for the action. Stockwell's history of his marriage and the birth of Belcour establishes a vital sentimental ground: distress and innocence. Innocence provides the necessary moral/sympathetic ground, and distress provides the need for moral action. With both innocence and need established as prior conditions, the myth is morally whole. Bevil reports Indiana's distresses: her shipwreck and the death of her mother, the death of her foster parents, her foster uncle's cruel lust and punishment of her. These reported events establish Indiana's innocence and need and elicit our automatic approval of Bevil. They provide sufficient emotional and moral justification and eliminate any need for further examination of either character or action.

5. Ibid.

Likewise, Stockwell reports his history and Belcour's to Hum-
phrey, who reacts with the astonishment and curiosity of a
Greek chorus. The exposition of the innocence/distress syn-
drome brings the plight of these merchants into a mythic context. Both character and action, in other words, can be explained; they have an origin, and myths tell stories of origin.
What is more, the facts of the origins are secrets, not shared
with everyone in the play. We the audience are privy to secrets
that will affirm clear moral divisions—who is deserving, who
is not; what partners belong together; who is just and righteous. Knowing those secrets puts the audience in the position of omniscient sympathy, and morality is felt rather than
thought.

Shaw and Brecht, in their polemics against the bourgeois
theater of the nineteenth and twentieth centuries, were ob-
jecting to the morality of feeling. Instead of being "guilty creatures sitting at a play" or being put into a position to judge an
action from a distance, the sentimental audience is brought
into the myth of morality through feeling. The "dreamers"
that Brecht described in "A Short Organum for the Theatre"
are entranced by their own feelings that seem identical to
those of the characters on stage.[6] The morality of feeling, however, begins in the eighteenth century.

Innocence and distress provide the moral drive to many a
comic plot. We presume, for example, that Viola in *Twelfth
Night* is innocent; her distress is clear in her first exchange
with the ship's captain. Shakespeare's plot, however, pro-
ceeds out and away from this moral ground. The shipwreck is
a prior condition, to be sure; it creates a need. Although we
sympathize with Viola's distress, we are more interested
through the play in how she solves her problem. We are keen
to witness her action and the development of the plot. Distress can be a structural device, in other words, creating a vac-
uum that needs to be filled with action. Obviously there is an
overlap between our sympathy and its moral ground and the

6. Bertolt Brecht, "A Short Organum for the Theatre," in *Brecht on Theatre*,
trans. John Willett (New York: Hill and Wang, Dramabook, 1957), p. 187.

structural development of a plot. In the sentimental comedy, however, innocence and distress are constantly reiterated so that we experience the moment of empathy with a dramatic character over and over again. The genre seems more concerned with the stasis of distress than with development, less interested in showing the skill and virtuosity of characters in solving their dilemmas than in creating moments of exquisite feeling. These are comedies of character rather than of action because the only skill required is innocence; their concerns are moral condition and constancy, subject matter rather than comic attitudes. Viola works her way through her problems with ingenuity and time ("O Time, thou must untangle this, not I"), so we sense a significant change through the course of the action. In the sentimental structure there is little sense of a new order. Instead, we sense the confirmation of an older, previously existing, order. Virtue and benevolence and highmindedness are rewarded for their constancy, not for their adaptibility. Peter Brooks has made a similar point in an article on melodrama as he compares it with comedy.[7]

The significance of the exposition in the sentimental comedy, then, is in some degree to validate the past, to locate in it the source of innocence and distress so that the future can affirm the original state of innocence. Thus the old society represented by the fathers does not so much block the path of the sons as test their characters. Like the melodrama, the sentimental comedy is concerned with testing virtue. The test of character reveals a great deal about the shared moral world of the two plays I am discussing. Stockwell, in the exposition to his servant Stuckely, reveals that he hopes "to make some ex-

---

7. Peter Brooks, "The Aesthetics of Astonishment," *Georgia Review* 30 (Fall 1976): 615. "What is being blocked in melodrama is very seldom the drive toward erotic union—so typically the case in comedy—which, if sometimes present, is no more than another indicator of virtue's right to reward. What is blocked, submerged, imprisoned is much more virtue's claim to exist qua virtue. Thus with the triumph of virtue at the end, there is not, as in comedy, the emergence of a new society formed around the uniting couple, ridded of the impediment represented by the blocking figure from the older generation, but rather a reforming of the old society of innocence which has driven out the threat of its existence and reaffirmed its values."

periment of my son's disposition." To do this, he plans to let "his spirit take its course without restraint" (1.1.11–14). The opening scene of *The Conscious Lovers* also reveals a father who has let his son live freely on his inheritance: "Now I thought liberty would be as little injurious to my son; therefore, as soon as he grew towards man I indulg'd him in living after his manner. I knew not how, otherwise, to judge of his inclination; for what can be concluded from a behaviour under restraint and fear?" (1.1.34–40). Each play sets out to prove not simply the virtue of the sons but the naturalness of that virtue. The fathers hope to see not just that their sons can live obediently, following the rules set down by their fathers and society, but that their righteousness is inherent, something that comes from their true nature, not from social training or authoritarian suppression. The benevolence and latitude the fathers offer their sons replicates the benevolence of the genial (as opposed to the wrathful Puritan) God toward his creatures. The tests by Stockwell and Bevil Senior thus duplicate the ideal of a social ethic based on divine order. Other comedies present the father as a rival and an obstacle to the son's fulfillment and thereby test the energy, imagination, and will of the son in real adversity. These fathers are far more benevolent. They represent that goodwilled Providence whose force will bring about all good things as long as human nature serves only goodness.

In each of these two plays, the goodness of the young heroes, Bevil and Belcour, has specific qualities. Its value is not simply based on the structural principle that the juvenile lead in a comedy has the sympathy of the audience and is always given the benefit of the moral doubt until proven unworthy. These heroes have more than structural value; they have "content." They enact the specific virtues of economic generosity, place little apparent value in money (that superfluous bit of ore), and display the unity of heart and hand. It is important that early in the play Belcour, hearing of Captain Dudley's plight, spontaneously offers the captain his two hundred pounds. For the audience Belcour establishes early his value as a generous, sympathetic character, so that later on we judge more kindly his error in using Charlotte's jewels to buy access to Louisa. Bevil's value is likewise established early through his undemanding support of Indiana and his prior rescue of her from the lustful, greedy clutches of her foster uncle. Both the heroes also acknowledge their duty and obedience to their father-benefactors. They share the correct balance of pride and humility, passion and reasonableness: each is willing to duel for the sake of his honor, but each acquiesces in the face of reasonable alternatives. They love passionately but respect the honor of women and marriage (unlike many of the Restoration rakes). Such virtuous principles and their enactment in the play create the content of virtue that characterizes the sentimental hero.

Yet the specific content of virtue is not the crucial element of the sentimental form. That form comes out of the idea that the value of a character is a commodity of the hidden interior, and plot joins the audience not with action or performance but with character. Even unsentimental heroes, in other words, make an appeal through the sentimental relation of audience and play. When Charles Surface in *School for Scandal* refuses to sell his uncle's portrait for any price, he demonstrates what I mean by the sentimental relation. His refusal proves his real worth, hidden by his rakish life-style. He shows both his uncle and the audience that in his character familial respect combines with a careless disregard for money; he acts freely, without the constraint of authority or reputation, thus demonstrating the naturalness of his virtues. His roguishness is simply the passionate spice added to his humanity. What is more, he contrasts significantly with his brother Joseph, who is a remnant of the Restoration rake, sans wit; who is all surface and form; and who seeks success without virtue. What had value in the Restoration plays seems villainous in sentimental plays. Although Charles Surface is not so consciously a sentimental hero as Bevil or Belcour, he creates the "liking" in the audience that has its origins in the sentimental value system. Like the sentimental hero, that is, Charles passes his test of character. The further distinction between Charles and Joseph, clearly, is that Charles is sincere:

he says what he means and he means what he says; Joseph, who speaks only for gain, is false and insincere: his interior is corrupt and the surface is all show. Even Oliver Goldsmith in his "laughing" comedy *She Stoops to Conquer* makes the principle of the interior truth and exterior show into a dialectic of character, and the action of the romantic plot is designed to reconcile the two aspects of young Marlowe.

The extension of inner truth and sincerity in character leads to realism. The sentimental hero does not come from romance, which is a consciously artificial form, but from the concerted effort to avoid artifice and to be as truthful as possible. By comparison with the sentimental hero, a Duke Orsino or an Orlando is a mere cipher. A Shakespearean lover may suffer and speak of the human pangs of love, but his value as a character is more thematic than morally specific. Orlando's place in the scheme of *As You Like It* allows us to assume his virtue; Orlando himself does not need to demonstrate continually his moral or ethical principles. Bevil and Belcour are not romantics, and it is no accident that they belong to the mercantile world. They do not live at a pastoral remove from city life but squarely in the center of urban mercantilism. City comedies as a rule tend toward satire, or at least they create a tension between the needs and impulses of individual appetites and the potentially corrupt demands of city life. But these two sentimental comedies conflate the values of character and those of the merchant society and in that conflation resolve the contradictions of wealth and worth. One must have money, but one must devalue it. The economic structure of the mercantile world is mythologized by the moral nature of character. To put it another way, the benevolence in a character veils the dichotomy of needing to have money in order to devalue money. Social values, economic values, and personal values are equivalent here, and the utilitarian aim of the plays is to suggest that paradise is concretely possible in the structures of society. The equivalence of personal and social values further conflates mythic perception and a social reality in which issues of money are tied to issues of the heart. Money is devalued as superficial dross, but it is never out of sight. The sentimental comedy demonstrates the conflated value of money and benevolence by a formulaic division between needy and needed characters. The downtrodden are essential to the sentimental formula. If there is to be benevolence, there must be objects worthy of it. Innocence and need apply to chaste heroines, to be sure, but generosity must be shown on the broader social scale as well or it might seem to be motivated by purely personal gratification. In *The West Indian* Captain Dudley and his family are both downtrodden and worthy. The captain, disinherited by his father-in-law, is willing to go to deadly regions of Africa to support his family, needing only two hundred pounds to equip himself for his commission. His self-sacrifice indicates that he is no mere beggar, no social leech. On hearing that Lady Rusport has refused him the two hundred pounds, the captain says: "That's hard; that's hard, indeed! My petition was for a small sum. She has refused it, you say? Well, be it so. I must not complain" (2.3.29–32). This beatitudinal meekness proves the true worth of the captain. His humility is the essential Christian component, and the play goes on to prove that the meek shall inherit, finally, old Sir Oliver's estate. Captain Dudley presents an opportunity for the play to verify specific Christian principles in an economic context. Behind the Dudley-Rusport plot, in other words, are some specific ethical aphorisms: God helps those who help themselves; The meek shall inherit the earth. These aphorisms are never spoken, but they are implicit in the moral perception of the action. They lie behind our approval of both Dudley's humility and his final success in receiving the estate.

The villains of the play are measured on an ethical scale tied to an economic base. Lady Rusport is thoroughly villainous not only because she refuses to help her relations with a small sum of money but because her heart is hard. She lacks the charity to forgive as well as the charity of her purse. She brings up the sins of her sister's past to excuse her own behavior and justifies her hardness on the authority of her father, who has disinherited the Dudley branch of the family. Lady Rusport's fault is an Old Testament one. She invokes the law of her father and uses the letter of the law to justify her own character faults.

Lest the tension of Lady Rusport's cruelty become too great, the play alleviates the effects of her harshness early on. She is seen for what she is by her suitor, Major O'Flaherty, by the end of act 2. He discovers and denounces her hard treatment of Captain Dudley and her ungenerous nature ("There isn't in the whole creation so savage an animal as a human creature without pity!" [2.11.35–37]). A human without Christian charity is no more than an animal. This early denouncement allows us to make a moral judgment long before the play is over. It defuses the particular tension of Lady Rusport's presence. This diffusion of tension says as much about the moral sensibility of the play as it says about structure. It may well be an effort to keep the moral tension from becoming too acute. Lady Rusport's plot over the will is disconnected from the action but is immediately connected to the fault of her character. The suppression of the will is simply another proof of her character; it is not structurally integrated from the beginning of the play.

Like the sentimental heroes, the sentimental villains carry a moral content that we can distinguish from the caricatured Vice figure. The cause of Lady Rusport's and the Fulmers' villainy is in their characters. These villains have no legacy from the traditional Vice figure who functions as an impersonal and motiveless goad to action. The sentimental villains bring the world of this play closer to that of melodrama and realism than to that of comedy. A more traditional Vice figure is as much a dramatic and theatrical energy as a moral representation. He needs no motive because he is almost the pure sign of trouble and mischief. He is largely impersonal and delights the audience with his self-conscious love of mischief for its own sake. He lies, cheats, steals, disrupts, and is virtually exempt from the efforts of society to contain him. His very distance from a personal sphere enables him to bring the audience into collusion with his malicious activities. In contrast, the villains of the sentimental comedies demonstrate specific errors of character, namely greed, hard-heartedness and a selfish disregard of others. The Vice figure can certainly exhibit similar attributes, but his moral and theatrical effect is different. We are never in danger of liking the sentimental villains and their maliciousness. The delightful danger of the traditional Vice figure is a significant element in the moral danger of comedy. His mobility between the world of the play and that of audience, his spontaneity and adaptability to circumstance, and his virtuosity are usually a delight to behold. From a moral point of view we do not necessarily condone him, but we enjoy his audacity and his freedom. Neither Lady Rusport nor the Fulmers are enjoyable in the same way. Their villainy rises out of the same moral fabric that gives good characters their goodness. They create no oscillation in the audience between attraction and repulsion, delight and condemnation, admiration and criticism. This oscillation is the genesis of comedy's moral ambiguity that attracts us even while it suggests moral impropriety. Moreover, the moral consciousness in the plays has lost the element of self-awareness that belongs to the Vice. The knowledge of good and evil that had been the special province of the Vice figure has been passed on to the sentimental hero, who is tested for his capacity to direct his nature toward the good.

Sincerity of character is transferred to sincerity of form. The sentimental form asserts its truthfulness and lack of artifice by calling on the sincerity of its intentions. It turns away from the ambiguity inherent in the conscious display and awareness of performance to the certainty that the world of the play represents a real world by simply asserting that it does. The moral project of the sentimental form implies the ontological sameness of fiction and reality and attempts to enclose the real world in its fiction. It is assertive insofar as it admits no dialectic of differences. For both *The Conscious Lovers* and *The West Indian* this moral project means that the interior world of the play and its values are identified with values in the real world. The plays reflect the sentimental ideal that values in human society, when founded on the natural virtue of human character, coincide with specific Christian virtues: charity, meekness, honesty, benevolence. One can simply refer to the beatitudes in Saint Matthew to find the character descriptions for these plays: the poor in spirit, they that mourn, the meek, they that hunger and thirst after righteousness, the merciful, the pure in heart, the peacemakers.

The impersonal contrivance that manipulates the shape of other comedy becomes, in sentimental comedy, the personal and benevolent action of Providence. We might say that the customary artificiality of comic form becomes the artfulness of Providence. It is no less "artificial," but it retains the notion of intentionality or consciousness in the driving action of plot. Both *The Conscious Lovers* and *The West Indian* attribute the outcome of the action to human goodness and a benevolent Providence. Compare the concluding speeches of the two plays:

> BELCOUR: I beseech you, amiable Louisa, for the time to come, whenever you perceive me deviating into error or offence, bring only to my mind the providence of this night, and I will return to reason, and obey.
> *The West Indian*

> SIR JOHN BEVIL: Now ladies and gentlemen, you have set the world a fair example. Your happiness is owing to your constancy and merit, and the several difficulties you have struggled with evidently show,
> Whate'er the generous mind itself denies
> The secret care of Providence supplies.
> *The Conscious Lovers*

The crucial conflict in both plays is a conflict of conscience, giving us a further sense that the site of the "real" action is interior. This site transfers directly from sentimental drama to the psychological arena of realism, where we are concerned with the multifaceted but hidden dimensions of the psyche. Our young sentimental heroes are not all goodness. They are aware that human nature can yield both to harmful passions and to generosity of heart. Belcour's first meeting with Stockwell testifies to his awareness that "passions" are his masters. Belcour's pursuit of Louisa through the streets of London suggests that he is not entirely free of "animal spirits," but his consciousness of those passions diffuses any serious moral threat to the goodness of his nature. The passions simply allow the demonstration of conflict in character, leading, ultimately, to obedience. We are allowed to forgive Belcour his passions, to see them as part of a "full" human nature as long as they never overwhelm the moral boundaries of generosity, the open heart, honor, and sincerity. Belcour's passions simply manifest his naturalness; they are purer in their way than the civilized politeness of the city. The natural man is naturally civilized (to recall Rousseau) and when tested without the restraint of authority, he proves his essential virtue. It is nature, finally, that binds the interior truth of feelings with the exterior show of language: sincerity is possible because it is "natural."

In obedience to Providence, which operates something like consciousness for nature, the hero finds success and happiness. Like nature, the Providence of sentimentality is immanent rather than transcendent. It offers happiness specifically in a social and economic paradise whose values are those of the family.[8] Action is aimed at simply giving sons and daughters a variety of opportunities to demonstrate the naturalness of their goodness to their fathers. The familial values transferred to the structure of comedy, under the umbrella of Providence, lead to a drama of character, not action. Jean-Paul Sartre puts it this way:

> [The] bourgeois theater does not want dramatic action. To put it more precisely, it does want dramatic action, but it does not

---

8. See Peter Szondi, "Tableau and *Coup de Theatre*: On the Social Psychology of Diderot's Bourgeois Tragedy," *New Literary History* 12 (Winter 1980): 323. The bourgeois tragedy, says Szondi, asks for predictability in its value structure, and that predictability is found in the values of the middle-class family of the "*interieur*," as opposed to the fickle court world, and the unpredictable reverses of fortunes and alliances in the struggle for power. The family is a permanent nucleus for charity and self-sacrifice: the source of personal values. Society, then, for the bourgeois sensibility, is necessarily the extension of the values of the nuclear family to the social "family of man." In the sentimental comedies, Providence is the divine version of the father of the family, caring for his children as long as they are reasonable, humble, dutiful, and sympathetic toward their fellows. It assures that all will be well if the children hold to their values.

want it to be human action, it does not want it to be the action of the man performing the play. It wants it to be the action of the playwright constructing a representation of itself that is subjective, that is to say, it wants to impose its own image of man upon the theater, one that conforms to its own ideology.[9]

One can also say of the sentimental comedy that when the artifice of performance is replaced by the construction of Providence, the voice of objectivity is lost. One version of that voice is the Vice figure that acknowledges the reality of "men performing the play." He represents the freedom of action that traverses the fictive world and the audience world, a remnant of the "lampooning mode" that puts comedy in the context of the immediate. A similar objectivity resides in the "asides" of Restoration drama, in the linguistic virtuosity of Shaw or Stoppard, or in the poetic artifice of Shakespeare and Jonson. This objectivity comes from the conspicuous artificiality of the devices of delight, and it creates an oscillation between fiction and reality. The delight of sentimentality, conversely, is meant to come from its moral content, not from its visible or auditory artifice. Since characters have moral content, they do not really need "acts" in Sartre's sense of the word. Certainly there are activities in the sentimental plot. There are good and bad deeds and a few obstacles. But there is none of what Sartre would call human action, because each deed is accompanied by its moral justification and explanation. Every action is bound not only by a moral code but also by the consciousness and expression of the code in speech. There is no tension, in short, between the social, economic, mythic, and human instincts and no assertion of human needs against the social background. The conspicuous lack of any biological or corporeal appetite eliminates any tension between desire and restriction. The desires of the body are displaced into an ethical code. Without the rupture of conflict either between the personal and the social or between moral action and aesthetic artifice, there is no evidence of what Sartre would call human freedom.

9. Jean-Paul Sartre, "Epic Theater and Dramatic Theater," in *Sartre on Theater* (New York: Random House, Pantheon Books, 1976), p. 92.

The appeal of the sentimental comedy is that of moral content in character. This comedy reaches out toward the subjectivity of the bourgeois or sentimental audience. As in melodrama, good and evil are easily distinguished, and no ambiguity arises. Sentimental comedy eliminates the friction between moral order and characters in action. We see not the performance of human contrariness and diversity but the action of Providence, the action of the Playwright behind the playwright that is ultimately the transcendent form of the subjective. The use of Providence as the final subjectivity confounds the spheres of immanent and transcendent action. If everyone lived in accord with true human nature, with an open heart toward others, the world would be perfect. The loss of any objective force—either moral or aesthetic—means that nothing ruptures the unity of the moral system or shows its failures or contradictions, so the plays rest in myth. With the expressed purpose to create a good example for their audience, the sentimental playwrights have refused to make the social world intelligible or the fictional world dangerously delightful. Oliver Goldsmith noticed this refusal in the eighteenth century:

> A new species of dramatic composition has been introduced under the name sentimental comedy, in which the virtues of private life are exhibited, rather than vices exposed; and the distresses rather than the faults of mankind make our interest in the piece. . . . If they [the characters] have faults or foibles, the spectator is taught not only to pardon, but to applaud them, in consideration of the goodness of their hearts; so that folly, instead of being ridiculed, is commended, and the comedy aims at touching our passions, without the power of being truly pathetic.[10]

Sentimental comedy, Goldsmith suggests, has taken over the pathetic aspects of tragedy and has lost the capacities of comedy to criticize and delight. For plays in which distress is the locus of delight and rescue is the example for instruction, the playwright asks the audience to invest a subjective pathos.

10. Oliver Goldsmith, "An Essay on the Theatre; or, A Comparison between Laughing and Sentimental Comedy," in *Collected Works of Oliver Goldsmith*, vol. 3, ed. Arthur Friedman (Oxford: Clarendon Press, 1966), p. 212.

When there is no comic rupture, the constituting elements of the social and moral fabric remain invisible. The aesthetic dimension of comic usefulness often begins at the rupture, not only because we see that rupture disturb the moral assumptions of the world of the play but because in our enjoyment of the disturbance we are morally ambivalent. In subjectivity, all contradictions are resolved: worth can both rest on wealth and despise money. Like a propaganda play, the sentimental comedy proves the validity of its moral structures; it delights in content and sets the example for the best in behavior.[11] But this idea of validity assumes that virtue and wickedness are absolutes of human nature, not attributes. As attributes, ethical features are subject to changing proportions; they can be tested for their limitations and ridiculed. The sentimental comedy leaves nothing open to ridicule. Among the comic utopias it is thus the most exemplary and the least comic. The happy ending gives us the form of comedy but not its function.

Comedy, unlike tragedy, is an optimistic form in spite of its capacity for bitterness and satire because it refuses to let the world rest in self-satisfaction. Tragedy at its best may create a joy in the acceptance of an absolute, but this absolute can never manifest itself in a social context, or it immediately becomes contingent; it must necessarily go beyond society into the realm of metaphysics and a personal confrontation with the absolute. Tragic heroes stand alone and may sacrifice themselves for their society, but they cannot take along any friend, for that friend would constitute a society and time would be introduced. Comedy belongs in time, in sequence, and in the contingency of a social world. Sentimental comedy consumes some of tragedy's timeless territory by making in-

11. Sartre, "Epic Theater," pp. 91–92. Sartre's term for such a play is "pessimistic naturalism." "This distaste for needs, this appearance of denying them, is precisely what I mean by pessimism. In other words, the bourgeoisie needs human nature simply in order to deny it. And moreover, if human nature is evil and eternal, it is quite obvious that no effort to make any sort of progress is required; or, to be fair, any progress there may be will be very slow. But in any case, obviously any description of nature will demonstrate that it will always remain the same in all circumstances."

distinguishable the personal, the social, and the metaphysical levels of moral action. Sentimentality, however, is not confined to the excesses of the sentimental comedy with its tender feelings and noble, selfless motives. Rather, it is a relation between a play and its audience that can occur at any time and in many dramas, whenever bourgeois values are seen as part of a natural law, whenever feelings combine forces with the "superfluous bit of ore," whenever the subjectivity of feelings in both play and audience confound the objectivity of a dramatic form, and whenever artifice becomes a transparency for the content of mercantile values. The extremity of the sentimental comedy shows most clearly what happens when moral content replaces the methodology of rupture. The delight of sentimentality is in identification, in the flow of subjectivity created by distress and benevolence in the embrace of Providence. This results in one form of comic satisfaction. It is unrelated, however, to the delight of rupture that turns a character or an event momentarily into an object, breaking the flow of subjective identification with the myth. Elements of sentimentality may well be found in Shakespeare, in the distress of shipwrecked children and long-lost fathers, in the happiness and success of lovers, in our care for and interest in his characters. But those elements are never reduced to the sphere of bourgeois certainty and the real world of a capitalist economy. They remain conspicuously in the realm of a romance myth and we delight in their distance from the mundane sphere. Sentimentality is the utilitarian method for mythologizing the mundane. As a consequence it loses the comic capacity for the criticism that makes society and human nature intelligible. In appealing to the brimming eyes and the bursting heart, it is no longer a comic response to the contradictions in human beings and society but a demand to feel, not think, to identify, not disengage.

6

Shaw's Paradox
Use in Dystopia

> I love the common people. I want to arm them against the
> lawyers, the doctors, the priests, the literary men, the pro-
> fessors, the artists, and the politicians. . . . I want a power
> simple enough for common men to use, yet strong enough
> to force the intellectual oligarchy to use its genius for the
> general good.
>
> Major Barbara

George Bernard Shaw is one of the few playwrights who explicitly and consistently tells us about the moral purposes of
his comedies. We can scarcely doubt his didactic intent. Indeed, the critic seeking insight into Shaw is frustrated because
Shaw is not very mysterious—he keeps no secrets—yet he is
elusive, so that most explanations seem incomplete. Even his
characters speak the language of the essayist: they make their
intentions clear at all points and we can never entirely separate the statements of Shaw's characters from his own. Cusins's speech, quoted in the epigraph of this chapter, has all
the marks of a defense of comedy.[1] It suggests that the moral
purpose of comedy is to arm "the common people" against
the authoritarian social figures who oppress them physically,
morally, and intellectually. No social idol is exempt from this
group of oppressors. It includes even the "literary men and
artists," presumably even Shaw himself, among those who
use their power for something other than "the general good."
Shaw might insist that he does use his power for the general

1. All quotations from *Major Barbara* are from *Bernard Shaw's Plays*, ed.
Warren S. Smith (New York: Norton, 1970). Subsequent quotations will be
given parenthetically in the text.

good and is thus excluded from the group of oppressors; he might also insist that any authority deserves to be knocked from its pedestal. But Shaw never tells us precisely what constitutes the general good, and critics expend much effort looking for the concrete social philosophy that the plays conceal. Shaw himself wrote so much critical exegesis in his various prefaces and has explained the moral concerns of his own plays so thoroughly that one tends to use Shaw the critic to explain Shaw the playwright. The critical thinker and the playwright are certainly close relations, but it is a mistake, I think, to let the Fabian socialist, philosopher, vegetarian, antivivisectionist, and defender of women's rights serve as sufficient interpreter for the playwright. The critical side of Shaw implies that a systematic philosopher resides behind the scenes. We look for consistency in a philosophy concerned with such specific issues as prison reform, religious oppression, slums, poverty, capitalism. But even if a play like *Major Barbara* contains such specifics (and it does) the consistency of the viewpoint is not made coherent by systematic thought. The consistency rather comes out of a principle of comic attitude—the attitude that takes any object for its material and inverts our perspective on it.

If we look for the concealed content of a statement like Cusins's, we may find none: it says what it means. If we ask what the general good is, we may well come to believe that Shaw is full of passionate intent but empty rhetoric. The form of the language implies philosophical content, and perhaps that philosophy can be stated in the lines that precede the quoted excerpt: "You cannot have the power to do good without having power for evil too." But this statement is less a coherent system than an attitude characteristic of one who sees paradox everywhere. If the sentimental comedy sets out to create a myth of social utopia, Shaw sets out to explode that myth with the perspective of paradox and the comic principle of inversion.

This is not to say that Shaw has no specific concerns or that no issues irritate him. His concerns, however, are sometimes at odds with the simple comic structure. *Major Barbara*, for ex-

ample, has a highly conventional structure that leads its characters to marriage and a new social integration. But the play
also appears to be concerned with specific social issues, so
that there is an ambivalent and precarious relation between its
ideational content and its aesthetically conventional form.
Shaw is an anomaly among comic playwrights because he
combines the broad principles of comic construction and attitudes with an apparently specific set of social irritants. Shaw,
unlike Jonson, however, does not find these irritants in human nature; and unlike Wycherley he does not find them in
social manners; instead they are in social structures. In his
preface to a collection of plays by Eugène Brieux, Shaw con-
veys his admiration as he states a significant principle of his
own perspective:

> Brieux wastes neither ink nor indignation on Providence. . . .
> When he sees human nature in conflict with a political abuse
> he does not blame human nature, knowing that such blame is
> the favorite trick of those who wish to perpetuate the abuse
> without being able to defend it. He does not even blame the
> abuse: he exposes it, and then leaves human nature to tackle it
> with its eyes open.[2]

The comic playwright who uses his comedy as social criticism starts with a perceived problem. Jonson begins with the
corrupt obsessiveness of human nature and human appetites,
Wycherley (less a social critic) with the manner of human in-
teractions, Shaw with the rational mind. For Shaw, social
structures are symptoms of the problem, not the source.
Shavian society is a product of human thought, however irrational, and its failures are the result of erroneous concepts.
Improvement comes not through the simple manipulation of
social institutions but in the reform of reason. We thus often
sense an attack, specific yet indirect, on social problems. Poverty is a genuine issue in *Major Barbara*, for example, but
Shaw's attitude of paradox throughout the play suggests that
the solution to poverty is an indirect one that does not lie in

---

2. George Bernard Shaw, Preface to *Three Plays by Brieux* (Cambridge,
Mass.: The University Press, 1907), pp. xvii–xviii.

the simple goodness of the Salvation Army. That simple goodness is merely an extension of the view that good and evil are
direct opposites and that goodness is the antidote for evil. The
naive view cannot perceive how evil is implicated in the good.
Reason or the ability to perceive complexity is directly connected to forms of social reality.

The social scene in Shaw is the evidence of the perceived
problem. We can see Shaw's connection to the naturalist and
realist playwrights of the nineteenth century, for whom the
scene functions as evidence or as the manifestation of a problem in moral perception. The structure of the plays follows the
structure of a scientific proof, as though "beginning, middle,
and end" were now "hypothesis, experiment, and proof."
The scene thus becomes an occasion for an analytic and diagnostic examination of society. Shaw takes his drama away
from the certainty of the naturalists, but he leaves their scene.

Francis Fergusson has suggested that Shaw "never found a
consistent comic convention" because "he did not distinguish
his aims from the realism of Ibsen."[3] His premise is that Shaw
takes up Ibsen's realistic form and intention and ignores the
comic convention in which the play presumes the presence of
the audience. As with Ibsen or Chekhov, the fourth wall stays
up at all times. Nothing breaks through it, nor does any Vice
figure move between the world of the play and that of the audience to bring audience and play into a shared aesthetic and
moral space. I suspect that Shaw replaces the Vice figure with
his own voice but will discuss the point later on. It is true,
however, that the intent of Shaw's plays is like that of Ibsen's.
In both, the scene is the evidence that the audience is invited
to examine from a distance, to watch through the lens of the
proscenium arch, and to judge. Ibsen makes his appeal for reform through pathos: however well Nora explains her departure, we first feel that she needs emancipation. Shaw appeals
to his audience through paradox, which from his viewpoint is
the form of thought that encompasses the broadest range of

3. Francis Fergusson, *The Idea of a Theatre* (Garden City, N.Y.: Doubleday,
Anchor Books, 1949), p. 191.

reality. The attitude, or perspective, of the comedian is para-doxical, and (we suspect) this attitude will keep social insti-tutions free from the corruptions of the one-eyed moralists. Shaw would arm the common man with two-eyed vision, even if that vision is contrary or inverted. With paradox, Shaw brings to naturalism a different form of social diagnosis. His comedy combines a world filled with bric-a-brac and moral zeal, and the audience is invited to believe that the moral premises are as solid as the settees.

In *Major Barbara*, Shaw takes us right to the settee. Lady Bri-tomart is at her writing table; it is after dinner in January 1906 at Wilton Crescent, London. "A large and comfortable settee is in the middle of the room, upholstered in dark leather." Shaw understands and communicates to the audience how these specifics signal a cosmic order as conceived and created by human beings. The household not only is realistic in detail, but also manifests the reality of a whole social system. The re-alistic scene attempts to disappear into familiarity, but it is nonetheless loaded with significance. The Britomart house-hold is as full of the order of the British cosmos as Under-shaft's Perivale St. Andrews is full of the fantasy of paradox. The Shavian scene is derivative in some degree: it comes out of the aesthetic of naturalism that discovers causality in the scene itself. Shaw recognizes the symbolic potential in the real. The room is also an idea of the room. Its details are si-multaneously themselves and more than themselves. If this play were by Ibsen, the room might be a prison; if by Strind-berg, it might be a festering womb; but because it is by Shaw, the room is the image of English domestic and moral econ-omy: it signals an order.[4] Moreover, it signals the historical tra-dition out of which its order arises, just as the name Lady Bri-tomart signals the tradition of English heroines in the allusion to Britomart in Spenser's *Faerie Queene*. The realism of the scene implies its own causality. Shaw uses this room con-

---

4. For a study on "rooms" in naturalism, see Bert O. States, "The Scenic Illusion: Shakespeare and Naturalism," in *Great Reckonings in Little Rooms: On the Phenomenology of Theater* (Berkeley: University of California Press, 1985).

sciously as the appropriate locale for Lady Britomart, who indeed conceives "the universe exactly as if it were a large house in Wilton Crescent" (p. 1).

The second act takes us to the yard of the West Ham Salvation Army shelter, and again the physical description functions as a moral perspective: "an old warehouse, newly whitewashed" (p. 18). It is a place, as Shaw describes it, where even the rich and comfortable would appear poor and miserable, and he thus recalls the naturalistic assumption that environment is a causal factor in human behavior. The whitewash is merely a thin covering for deep grime and poverty; Zola might have appreciated such an environment. The third act takes us briefly back to the Britomart household and then to the munitions factory at Perivale St. Andrews, "an almost smokeless town of white walls, roofs of narrow green slates or red tiles, tall trees, domes, campaniles, and slender chimney shafts, beautifully situated and beautiful in itself" (p. 56). This is an image of a heavenly city lying between two Middlesex hills: pure, clean, beautiful, airy, and light. It is also, of course, a paradoxical scene, for Shaw makes the physical scene invert our sense of the moral scene, and what he achieves is a sense of the paradox of the real.

In brief, Shaw uses settings emphatically, not accidentally. They create around the action a silent causality that does indeed suggest the realistic worlds of Ibsen, Strindberg, Chekhov, Scribe, Brieux, Robertson. But these realists would most likely not have introduced the white-walled Mediterranean heaven in Middlesex even ironically. St. Andrews is a scene of romance and belongs in the world of comedy, not in that of tragedy, realism, or domestic melodrama. Shaw undermines the substantive objects—a cannon, a powder shed, and mutilated straw corpses—with the clean, fresh, and expansive qualities of the scene. He makes a similar shift of scene in *Man and Superman* when he takes us to Spain, and in *Too True to Be Good* when he sends the action to the sea beach in a mountainous country or, by extension of the principle, when he brings Saint Joan back to the Dauphin's chamber. For Shaw does seem to suggest the world of the naturalists and to take their social concerns for his own; he appears to offer the same assumptions about society and a similar diagnosis of its ills; but then he disorients us with a sudden dislocation of scenes, bringing in the unlikely, the romantic, the fantastic. His scenes are at first much like Ibsen's, perhaps because of his confessed admiration for Ibsen, but the romantic comedian then breaks out of the domestic prisons.

It may be, on the other hand, that the intentions of the naturalists found a place in the comic convention of locating action in the mundane world and in its capacity for criticizing that world. Realistic melodramas may be seen as comedies that have turned pathetic by an excessive infusion of sympathy rather than of ridicule; the critical eye of naturalism may not be as objective as it pretends, for it is often clouded by the sympathetic judgment of how things ought to be. Comedy is the genre in which objectivity finds a natural habitat, and Shaw was able to bring into the realm of comedy what he admired in the New Drama. "In the new plays, the drama arises through a conflict of unsettled ideals rather than through vulgar attachments, rapacities, generosities, resentments, ambitions, misunderstandings, oddities and so forth as to which no moral question is raised. The conflict is not between clear right and wrong: the villain is as conscientious as the hero, if not more so."[5]

Ibsen and Shaw may share a distrust of the simple divisions between right and wrong, good and evil that dominated the melodramas of the nineteenth century, and they may share the idea that drama ought to be instrumental in changing the moral perceptions of its society; but they differ insofar as Ibsen's judgments are fundamentally pathetic and appeal to our sympathies and Shaw's judgments are rational and appeal to our minds. Shaw revels in unsettled ideals, even his own.

Paradox, in short, is Shaw's moral instrument; and he uses it not only in the ideas presented by his plays and their characters but also in the aesthetic devices of language and struc-

5. George Bernard Shaw, "The Quintessence of Ibsenism," in *Major Critical Essays*, vol. 19 (New York: Wm. Wise, 1931), pp. 149–50.

ture. *Major Barbara* is a clear example of the perspective of paradox that functions as both a structure and a moral instrument, that is, in both utilitarian and aesthetic ways. Fergusson points out that if one reads *Major Barbara* as a thesis play, it seems to say that the munitions factory (and by extension the whole capitalist system) is the way of salvation; Shaw's point, of course, is heavily ironic.[6] But Shaw presses the point far beyond the simple tongue-in-cheek irony that he does not really mean what he has proven. At one level, we can say that he is demonstrating a contradiction between the desire of idealists to do good in the world and the capacity of realists to effect good. Barbara's best intentions cannot fund the Salvation Army; principles aside, the money of her father the munitions maker keeps the outpost going. In the clearest possible way, Undershaft convinces Barbara and the audience that his death-dealing instruments of war are the fountain of social good. He proves to us that the real evils of hunger and poverty, and the moral ills they create in characters like Bill Walker, are redeemed not by good intentions but by real deeds, and real deeds tend to be dirty ones. Social good, found in Perivale St. Andrews, comes when poverty is eliminated and the hypocrisy of idealism is dissolved.[7] The munitions factory is the reality principle that all members of the family learn to accept, though in acceptance they must give up the claims of inheritance (Stephen), of legitimate birth (Cusins), of self-righteous principles (Lady Britomart), and of religious idealism (Barbara). Shaw flagrantly violates the rule

6. Fergusson, *Idea of a Theatre*, p. 193.

7. Undershaft states the paradox most clearly when he says in *Major Barbara*: "I had the strongest scruples about poverty and starvation. Your moralists are quite unscrupulous about both: they make virtues of them. I had rather be a thief than a pauper. I had rather be a murderer than a slave. I dont want to be either; but if you force the alternative on me then, by Heaven, I'll choose the braver and more moral one. . . . Poverty and slavery have stood up for centuries to your sermons and leading articles: they will not stand up to my machine guns. Dont preach at them: dont reason with them. Kill them" (p. 66). The play does not enact this violence: that would be too brutal for Shaw. As long as the idea of violence can remain an idea in the form of a rational paradox, he can appear a radical revolutionary without taking the consequences (aesthetically as well as actually) of revolution.

that comedy must punish the wicked and reward the virtuous. His comedy is based on the impossibility of separating
the wicked from the virtuous. He goes to great lengths not
just to implicate good in evil and make them indistinguishable
but also to say, in essence, that evil creates good and good is
powerless unless it embraces evil. Such a conclusion is an outrageous rupture of the moral fabric, for it suggests not simply
that good and evil must coexist but that good and evil are perfectly inverted. Shaw proves the inversion with perfect clarity
and logic. So when Undershaft saves the Salvation Army post
with his check, when he brings Cusins into the family fold
("Six o'clock tomorrow morning, Euripides"), we both know
and feel that there is no difference between selling out to evil
and embracing a social good.

At last theoretically, it is reasonable to use paradox as a corrective instrument. Such a use is intentionally unsettling and
disrupts the surface of conventional morality, unexamined
certainties, and thoughtless platitudes. Paradox is an immediately dialectic form that ruptures the cohesion sympathy
creates. Brecht turned the paradox into a mainstay of *Verfrem-
dungseffekt*: it ensured a critical social attitude toward events
and situations. It threw the "problem" of the play not onto the
characters to solve but onto the audience to evaluate, as, for
example, when the gods in *The Good Woman of Setzuan* take
their leave, refusing to settle the dilemma of the good person/
bad capitalist identity crisis, and will not answer the woman's
immediate moral question. Brecht's moral is explicit: "It is for
you, my friends [the audience], to help good men arrive at
happy ends." Argument, debate, contradiction, paradox:
through these elements, not through sympathies, feelings, instincts, situations are made intelligible. And from the basis of
intelligibility men are able to make the ethical judgments from
which to effect moral change in the world. Brecht and Shaw
have in common their concern with the ethos of human action
and their sense that morality is not a God-given but humanly
determined system. By the right application of intelligence, it
appears possible to eliminate the social evils of poverty or
hunger.

The methodology of intelligence, however, tends to conceal

its ideals. Shaw delights in his contradictions; he revels in the disturbance of the peace. He refuses to let us know what he thinks because his own skill at dialectic could overturn even his own assertions. All opinions are assailable in the Shavian world, but it is a closed world because in it there is nothing but opinions. That the "way of life" should be through the "factory of death" is an apparent absurdity; can Shaw really mean it? Certainly not a man of his apparent moral scruples. But this absurdity is one whose satisfactoriness is shocking. As Shaw himself said, there are neither villains nor heroes in his plays. For him the really interesting questions are, who are the villains and who the heroes? and by what system of thought do we decide which is which? The only way out of the closed world of Shavian opinions that are all equal (as Barbara says, "There is no wicked side; life is all one") is a leap into fantasy. The munitions factory is a fantastical place, as is Don Juan's hell, the seaside resort in a mountainous country, and heartbreak house. Shaw's paradoxical habits and his opinionated assertiveness combine to create a restless play of ideas that appear solid but are chimeras for an almost sentimental sense of human nature. Indeed, his loftier view of the world seems almost mystic in its assertion of unity: that "life is all one" enables Barbara to accept all contradictions, to do the wrong thing for the right reasons, or vice versa.

The critical eye sees the failure of the world to measure up to the ideal. And Shaw sees this failure primarily as a lack of intelligence in others. Pirandello perceived the contradiction in the collision of Shaw's ideals and his view of reality.

> Whenever, instead of tolerating, instead of pitying, he loses his temper at the shock of reality against his ideals, and then, for fear of betraying his anger—which would be bad mannered—begins to harass himself and his hearers with the dazzling brilliancy of his paradoxes, Shaw, the artist properly speaking, suffers more or less seriously—he falls to the level of the jeu d'esprit which is amusing in itself, though it irremediably spoils the work of art.[8]

8. Luigi Pirandello, "Bernard Shaw's *Saint Joan*," reprinted in *Bernard Shaw's Plays*, p. 448.

Shaw's refusal to resolve his paradoxes may indeed confuse both the instrumentality and the aesthetic of his plays. In *Major Barbara*, Shaw leads up to a comic paradox, so that at the moment it is spoken, we know we are at the heart of his concern, but he empties the moment with the virtuoso display of verbal energy and dissolves any content. Major Barbara, having first lost her faith in the Salvation Army and then regained it with the new wisdom of Undershaft, says, "There must be some truth under all this irony." The comment might well apply to Shaw's methodology. Like the notion of the Life Force, Shaw's comedy seems to have content, seems to imply some propositional truth under all the irony, but finally is primarily an effect, not a substance. Comedy does not have to take up serious social issues or have serious content, of course, but Shaw implies that he is serious. He claims to be a revolutionary and indeed recognizes comedy as an efficacious form of revolution. "All very serious revolutionary propositions begin as huge jokes. Otherwise they would be stamped out by the lynching of their first exponents."[9] This position is essentially the same as that of Jeremy Collier or Stephen Gosson, who also hold that drama, and comedy in particular, is subversive and dangerous because it gives the semblance of harmlessness.

The subversiveness of comedy, that is, is not so simple that it just sets a bad example of behavior. There is no necessary connection between what a play portrays and what members of the audience will do in imitation. The deeper subversiveness of comedy, and perhaps of art forms in general, is that they open new possibilities for thought and behavior—they

---

9. Shaw, "The Quintessence of Ibsenism," p. 136. Shaw goes on to elaborate the principle of revolution through jokes with the following story: "Two friends of mine, travelling in remote parts of Spain, were asked by the shepherds what their religion was. 'Our religion,' replied one of them, a very cultivated author and traveller, with a sardonic turn, 'is that there is no God.' This reckless remark, taken seriously, might have provided nineteenth century skepticism with a martyr. As it was, the countryside rang with laughter for days afterwards as the stupendous joke was handed round. But it was just by tolerating the blasphemy as a joke that the shepherds began to build it into the fabric of their minds."

create an apparently new space for thought by rupturing the "fabric of the mind." What is opened up by an absurdity can be explored as a possibility at leisure. The danger of a new thought or a new form is that it does change the world: it adds to the vocabulary of potential that then redefines the actual.

Shaw consistently claims his revolutionary status in the voices of characters like Undershaft or Cusins or Saint Joan or Jack Tanner who preach to the audience under the thinnest disguise as characters. But like most revolutionaries Shaw is a romantic who sees the real world as a "hard" place—a dystopia where the failure of intelligence prevents the achievement of perfection on earth and in society. But since the application of intelligence is an ongoing process, any given set of circumstances is susceptible to a dialectic razor. There is no state or condition that would be acceptable to Shaw—except perhaps the imaginary creations of his fancy—for such a state would not need his mind, his energy, or his verbosity. The failures of the world are happy occasions for Shaw because they are opportunities to show his virtuosity, like the revolutionary so self-consumed that he creates resistance where there is none, simply to perpetuate his status as revolutionary. So just when Shaw would be subversive, he turns out to be simplistic; in part because his principle of inversion is so symmetrical. When Cusins concludes that "the way of life lies through the factory of death," we are on the level of an almost simple-minded irony—or at least an adolescent irony. Shaw is not undermining our assumptions in any subversive or subtle way; he does not make us doubt: in the first place, his terms are too sweeping; in the second, his enthusiasm is too overpowering. Heaven, he suggests, can invert hell, making it all one. In reply to Cusins's statement, Barbara says,

> Yes, through the raising of hell to heaven and of man to God, through the unveiling of an eternal light in the Valley of The Shadow. . . . Oh, did you think my courage would never come back? did you believe that I was a deserter? that I, who have stood in the streets, and taken my people to my heart, and talked of the holiest and greatest things with them, could ever turn back and chatter foolishly to fashionable people about nothing in a drawing room?
>
> (pp. 72–73)

Barbara's revelation is apocalyptic but undramatic. Her conversion is simply redirected piety, for it is not the action but the argument that has changed her. Knowledge, for Shaw, is not experience but intelligence: St. Andrews is just the concrete proof of Undershaft's argument. Barbara's change is no moral conversion, it is a rhetorical inversion that has only the appearance of moral content: and the rhetorical play of words is, for the most part, an ironical comment on the comic-romance structure of the play. In a speech like Barbara's, we see Shaw bringing Nietzsche into the drawing room of fashionable people, as though the veil of illusion could be lifted from the house on Wilton Crescent. What is thoroughly paradoxical in Shaw is not the philosophical paradox of a world beyond good and evil but the placement of that paradox in the trappings of nineteenth- and twentieth-century domestic and social economy.

The paradoxical discussions of opinions in *Major Barbara* conceal its romance structure. The play does indeed move toward the "ritual" marriage of Barbara and Cusins, the "discovery" of the foundling child, the apparent reconciliation of the older couple. Undershaft even fulfills the function of the "blocking" father figure. The play certainly suits Northrop Frye's definition of comic structure:

> The society emerging at the conclusion of comedy represents . . . a kind of moral norm, or pragmatically free society. . . .
> Thus the movement from *pistis* to *gnosis*, from a society controlled by habit, ritual bondage, arbitrary law and older characters to a society controlled by youth and pragmatic freedom is fundamentally, as the Greek words suggest, a movement from illusion to reality. Illusion is whatever is fixed and definable, and reality is best understood as its negation: whatever reality is, it's not *that*.[10]

Shaw keeps the fundamental structure of comedy and simply inverts the society: the youthful generation lives with illusions (probably passed on through Lady Britomart) and is

---

10. Northrop Frye, *Anatomy of Criticism* (Princeton, N.J.: Princeton University Press, 1957), pp. 169–70. Frye goes on to point out that the ending of *Major Barbara* is a "brilliant parody of a *cognitio*."

taught pragmatic freedom by the older generation (Undershaft). The conventional morality that appears to be the object of Shaw's attack is in bondage to habit and arbitrary law. Many of Shaw's plays lead to marriage or toward reconciliation, but romantic/poetic justice is always won at the price of discussion. In each case, habit is broken down by the power of a fresh pragmatic rationale. Shaw allows Barbara the conventional marriage for unconventional reasons. He seems to want to offer us the best of both romance and criticism, suggesting that the happy ending could be rational and the moral norm could be reasonable, not romantic. Just as Candida's justification for staying married to Morell is pragmatic (or paradoxical: he is the weaker of the two) and antiromantic, so too is Anne Whitefield's rejection of Tavy on the principle that his romantic ideals are impossible to maintain in reality, or the "Sergius principle" that the higher love is very difficult to keep up for any length of time. But in spite of these proofs of antiromantic hardheadedness, Shaw offers the audience the satisfactions of the comic romance: Jack does end up with his Jill, even if Shaw's own ethical perversity has distorted the sentimental obliviousness of conventional romance. In attempting to satisfy both the heart and the head, Shaw serves us another illusion: that the conventional romance can be confirmed and supported by reason. One could also see Shaw's intent as precisely the opposite: that the ethical discussions demonstrate the arbitrariness and absurdity of romance conditions, so we laugh at that very arbitrariness. But perhaps both conclusions ignore the possibility that Shaw simply used the conventional structure of comedy to display his more immediate interest in verbal virtuosity and paradox. The content of the Shavian fictional world seems secondary to the attitudes and energy of the Shavian voice.

Shaw's voice in his plays is ever present, but that presence is musical as much as ideological. The operatic allusions, the combination of characters as voices (tenor, soprano, bass), the order of scenes (overtures, arias, duets, and ensembles), the bravura performances of the speech makers, and the musical scoring of speeches by key signature, tempo, and musical dynamics: all are well-documented aspects of Shaw's dramatic construction.[11] It is somewhat difficult, however, to reconcile the musical nature of the plays with the drama of ideas that we associate with Shaw. If music is the most extreme form of emotional, nonreferential, noninformational communication, how does it carry the rational discourse and logical content of the drama of ideas?[12] The contradiction is similar to that of the romantic structure as it contradicts the ethical dialectics of Shaw's thought: in both the structure and the dialectic the emotional force is not of the same quality as the rational force, and it is difficult to know which one persuades us in favor of the play. We can say that for Shaw ideas carry passion and that he creates characters who feel ideas with the same intensity that most humans feel emotions. It is customary to imagine ideas as containers with rational contents and feelings as atmospheric and irrational impulses, but Shaw does not appear to divide passion from thought. His discussions are not wholly rational, and it is not their content, finally, that interests us and captures our attention but our own inability to distinguish in them the power of sound from the power of ideas. The content alone—the reduced ironies that come out of the virtuoso displays—is minor indeed: the way of life is through the factory of death. Shaw builds his speeches from pure sound as Shakespeare builds his speeches with images: they grow before us and collect around them the illusion of more content than is actually present. Shaw's language is developmental, like music. One statement leads to the next and cre-

11. See the chapter by Martin Meisel, "Opera and Drama," in *Shaw and the Nineteenth Century Theater* (Princeton, N.J.: Princeton University Press, 1963).
12. Ibid., pp. 59–60. "In revolting against 'a genus of opera without music,' the drama of pure emotion, Shaw committed himself to a species of drama much more musical in its fundamental nature: the drama of ideas. For 'If you want to produce anything in the way of great poetic drama,' he declared, 'you have to take a theme, as Beethoven did in his symphonies, and keep hammering at the one theme.' As Shaw developed from his first explorations of popular genres to the full-fledged Discussion Play, he become more and more adept at the development and counterpointing of ideas as if they were musical themes."

ates a continuing, ever-enlarging environment of ideas that are joined almost organically.

The language of *Major Barbara* is aphoristic in its assertion and aggression. Certainly no major character ever appears unsure of himself; so consistent is this self-assurance (even when unwarranted) that it becomes the signal for Shaw's own voice. The tone may change from character to character as from soprano to tenor or bass, but the style of the music is all Shavian. And because speeches are built musically as much as rationally, it becomes almost impossible to cut out any phrase without changing the shape of the speech. And any speech can serve as an example:

> I was an east ender. I moralized and starved until one day I swore that I would be a full-fed free man at all costs; that nothing should stop me except a bullet, neither reason nor morals nor the lives of other men. I said "Thou shalt starve ere I starve"; and with that word I became free and great. I was a dangerous man until I had my will: now I am a useful, beneficent, kindly person. That is the history of most self-made millionaires, I fancy. When it is the history of every Englishman we shall have an England worth living in.
>
> (p. 66)

This speech has the feel of the aphorism without the form. One of the difficulties with Shaw, in fact, is that one cannot cut off his phrases, cannot pare down the plays, for no single part contains the whole. We need the entire speech to complete the idea, and even then that speech depends on further speeches for musical balance. Shaw is as efficient as he can be, for finally the musical elaboration of passionate ideas, not reductive content, determines the form. The fictional world of Shaw appears to have content because it is built by language in the indicative mood. The mood of the language, furthermore, implies that there is reality in the Shavian world.

The build of the Shavian speech and scene is an aesthetic dimension that makes us forget the intentionality of the speeches themselves. That dimension conceals the outrageous position of Undershaft (as though freedom of mind leads everyone to riches) by creating admiration for the marvelously logical structure, the eloquence of the connections, and the build of the proof. We suspect that Undershaft cannot be "right" in a moral sense, even if we have to accept the reality of his position: that the best of intentions do not eliminate poverty and hunger, that the most sympathetic concern for the individual does not feed him. The power of the rhetoric keeps us from examining the content too closely, and though we might be outraged, we are nonetheless convinced—that is, astonished and delighted at the cunning impossibility and the audacity of the position—because the musicality of the language disconnects our admiration from our moral ground. The speech makes assertions, but we are swept away by the passion of the concerns, not the concerns themselves. We become fascinated by the paradox as a structure, regardless of its content. We may not remember what a character has said, but we remember he said it marvelously. Just as the music of an opera tells us the emotional content of a moment without our necessarily understanding Italian or German or English, we feel Shaw's speeches through the dynamics of the speech. And just as an opera can become mundane and trivial when we know that the tenor is only calling for a glass of water— that is, when it is translated into a familiar language—so Shaw's ideas can seem trivial or simplistic when they escape the musical carriers of his plays. For the music in the speeches carries the comic attitudes we come to appreciate, and attitudinizing makes many of the characters funny as well as likable. All of Shaw's characters are sophists in some degree, insofar as the style of their rhetoric enables them to present outrageous positions.

In Shaw's plays that have neither villains nor heroes, neither vices to be punished nor virtues to be rewarded, the moral norm emerges from the element of musicality. We cannot divide characters into moral camps or identify the good, the bad, or the ugly. The norm, rather, is presented by the attitude of "good sense" that comes out of a balanced perception, combined with the courage and bravery with which characters assert their positions. Undershaft's scruples are audacious: he would rather be a murderer than a slave; it is the braver and more moral choice. If there is a typical Shavian heroic gesture, it might be the lone individual on stage flinging defiant absurdities to the gods, and the verbal mode of this gesture is Shaw's audacious musicality. We admire it not simply for its content but for its courage. Shaw's language is styled to infect the audience with his own enthusiasms, not to let it examine his premises. He pretends he wants us to think about moral conventions and the structures of society that create evils like poverty, hunger, prostitution, or war, but above all he seems to want us to admire the courageous individual who will stand against the outrages of society in an outrageous stance. Undershaft is such a character and his argument converts all the other characters as well as the audience to the belief that a munitions factory can create a little utopia.

Undershaft is also a normative character because he appears to hold mutually exclusive perspectives in simultaneous view. As a character he is a paradoxist. In Shaw, single-minded characters are the aberrations. Lady Britomart, though charming in her way, is the kind of adamantine moralist that Shaw loves to topple. It is Undershaft who can say on entering his family fold after many years: "My difficulty is that if I play the part of a father, I shall produce the effect of an intrusive stranger; and if I play the part of a discreet stranger, I may appear a callous father" (p. 12). There is moral as well as rhetorical balance in this sentence. And just because Undershaft sees the reverse of each possible posture, he is immediately appealing. This capacity for reversed perspectives appears here in the cloak of humility, but later the same capacity will enable Undershaft to disprove Barbara's false god and offer salvation through munitions. The reversal of positions based on the principle of inversion is thus a habit that we have come to trust by the time Undershaft shows off his little utopia. The lessons of the play, in fact, have more to do with characters' assimilating the attitude of paradox and contradiction than with their accepting the moral content of a proposition.

This assimilation is especially funny when we see a character like Lady Britomart, overwhelmed with St. Andrews, accepting the conditions *de facto* but maintaining her own posture rhetorically. "Charles Lomax: you are a fool. Adolphus Cusins: you are a Jesuit. Stephen: you are a prig. Barbara: you are a lunatic. Andrew: you are a vulgar tradesman. Now you all know my opinon; and my conscience is clear, at all events" (p. 68). She silently acknowledges the benefits of the factory and clears her conscience by stating her opinion. In doing this she is both very funny and acceptable to the audience, for she has become part of the norm that integrates or at least holds contradictory positions. The paradox or contradictory position is the basis of Shaw's methodology of intelligence.

The Shavian voice that rings out in the language and the perspective of paradox is a voice of passionate intelligence. This voice insists on its right to be contrary, if not self-contradictory, like the Vice figure of the traditional morality play. What I have been calling the musicality of the play is also a nonnaturalistic feature that reaches out beyond the fourth wall of the realistic stage illusion. The language continually points at Shaw himself as the creator of the action. Shaw emerges to speak directly to the audience, just as the Vice figure emerges in character from the fictional world of the morality play to speak directly to the audience of his intentions, his prospects for dirty deeds, his manipulation of the action. Both the Vice as character and the voice as Shaw are overt aesthetic and moral devices. The passion of the speech belongs to Shaw himself. Whenever we become conscious of an overt aesthetic device (whether in language or in character), the art form breaks out of its simple significative role. The overt device produces a collaborative effort of audience, maker, and work by rupturing the connection between word and meaning, form and subject, sign and signification.[13] The poetic de-

13. In the theater, Brecht used overt devices of theatricality to create the critical distance between actor and audience that put the audience in a position of judgment rather than identification. A related "alienation" effect is described in linguistic terms in Sigurd Burckhardt, *Shakespearean Meanings* (Princeton, N.J.: Princeton University Press, 1968), p. 24: "I propose that the

vice—in Shaw's case, the combination of the paradox with his rhetorical music—severs the denotative connection and, by extension, the moral connections between statement and truth, so that we end up with an appearance of assertion without the substance of assertion. Aubrey's sermon at the end of *Too True to Be Good* is a case in point. Aubrey says he cannot help going on preaching no matter how late it is; we almost lose the substance in his passion. Shaw's own comment is that "fine words butter no parsnips." The sermon loses all personal character and is severed from the play. Similarly, the emergence of a Vice character from a play dissociates the representational from the presentational nature of the actor and disrupts the presumed identification of actor and character. The dissociation brings the human being into focus as both a medium and a subject matter that exists in the mode of pure performance. So Shaw's language is a disguise that barely covers the nonsignifying and nonrepresentational status of his statements. We may be charmed by the Shavian characters, but the plays point inevitably toward Shaw the creator. Just as we go to a symphony to hear Beethoven or Mozart, not particular woodwinds or brass sections, we go to hear Shaw more than to see his play and characters. His characters are merely the instruments for his voice. As one reviewer complained about a production of *The Apple Cart*: "Action has totally disappeared and all the characters sit on chairs, hour in and hour out. And in the place of human emotion is the brain of Shaw, bulging larger and larger, filling the stage, hard and brilliant, glittering like a jewel."[14] Shaw's own voice takes the audience away from the realistic illusion of the stage pictures. His musicality constitutes the aesthetic and moral freedom that en-

---

nature and primary function of the most important poetic devices—especially rhyme, meter and metaphor—is to release words in some measure from their bondage to meaning, their purely referential role, and to give or restore to them the corporeality which a true medium needs. To attain the position of creative sovereignty over matter, the poet must first of all reduce language to something resembling material."

14. F. R. Bellamy, quoted in Stanley Weintraub, "The Avant-Garde Shaw," in *Bernard Shaw's Plays*, p. 351.

ables him to break through the fourth wall and to function simultaneously in the world of the characters onstage and in the world of the audience, incorporating these worlds in the same moral space, even while he allows the play to operate structurally in a romance illusion. But certainly this voice makes plays that are filled with talk. The language has the assertive quality of true statements that are simply inverted to turn our conventions around ("My best friend is my bravest enemy").

Shaw does not fit easily in a category of either dystopia or utopia. In *Major Barbara*, both the final version of St. Andrews and the musical energy of the language suggest a utopian vision that resides in the work itself, if not in a represented reality. The devices of delight, in other words, suggest that Shaw's works are related to an aesthetic idealization. One could easily argue for Shaw's utopian vision. On the other hand, Shaw needs the idea of a dystopian world to begin his discussion. He needs the image of a dystopia that is created by the obdurate persistence of unexamined moral self-assurance. The world is dystopian not because it is evil but because it is monolithic. In *Major Barbara*, it is a social monolith because moral certainty like Lady Britomart's or, for a time, Barbara's creates and helps to perpetuate specific social evils. The dystopia of moral certainty gives Shaw the occasion for his discussion and for the play of his rhetoric and allows him the posture that his work is socially useful. That sense of utility may be at odds with the vision of a utopia manifested in Shaw's verbal play. A social satirist meets social evils on their own ground and tries to match the energy of the world he satirizes with the energy of his corrective ridicule. Shaw uses his paradoxical habit not viciously but genially. Unlike the satirist who implies a division between right and wrong, Shaw attempts to go beyond these moral categories to suggest a division between morality and reality. The world of conventional morality is the dystopian world of illusion; the realist goes beyond good and evil but discovers a reality that seems in its own way utopian. Shaw's realism in *Major Barbara* suggests that the drawing-room world of Lady Britomart can transcend the contradiction of good and evil and that the veil of illusion can be lifted. Nietzsche turns into Charles Lomax, who says innocently, "There is a certain amount of tosh about this notion of wickedness. . . . Not that I would say a word in favor of anything wrong; but then, you see, all sorts of chaps are always doing all sorts of things; and we have to fit them in somehow, dont you know" (p. 67). Through the impossible tension of a rational paradox, such reasonable characters as Barbara, Cusins, and Undershaft make an irrational leap to the imaginary world beyond good and evil and create the larger fantasy of a rational utopia. And finally, for Shaw, utopia is most likely a play: a place of paradox and discussion in which he can go on talking indefinitely, never coming to rest in a specific social world. For though Shaw is socially motivated, he is metaphysically concerned and is constantly making judgments *sub specie aeternitatis*. Utopia and dystopia, then, constitute another paradox in Shavian terms, for the presence of a dystopia makes the projection of a utopia necessary, and finally Shaw seems to want to correct that dystopia through his utopian vision.

The further problem of Shaw's combination of social and metaphysical attitudes and his habit of covering all bases with paradox is that he essentially leaves no room for error. He may indeed demonstrate that "there is no wicked side: life is all one," but in so doing he betrays an attitude much like that of the sentimental comedy. Shaw ruptures the fabric of morality, unlike the sentimentalists, and shows the contradictions of any moral stance, but then he covers that rupture with a unifying canopy of metaphysical wholeness that takes his comedy out of the social world into the divine. That unity tends to destroy the humor in an immediate situation and leads us to imagine the genial laughter of the gods. In his dialectic Shaw always insists on the larger perspective, and this perspective takes the plays out of the immediately human realm. The further difficulty is not that the audience is forced to think rather than feel but that the thinking has been done already for them. There is really nothing left for an audience to do: Shaw does not trust his audience enough to let them perform their function, which in a comedy is to cooperate and collaborate on the jokes, on the perspective, on the filling in of the excluded moral structure. Shaw delivers it all. He leaves no room for error in his arguments because he inevitably keeps them going. He asks the audience only to listen to what he has to say—to be passive receptors. Certainly he offers us heaven and hell, the social and the divine, and he delights us with his rhetorical performance, but he finally ignores us and our function.

The irony of Shaw's "unresolved paradox" is that it creates a monolithic aesthetic form that reflects, in a way, the very dystopian monolith of moral certainty that the plays presume to correct. There is no place in a Shavian play for an alternative perspective. The perfect symmetry of Shaw's principle of inversion defines the terms and perpetuates them as virtual absolutes. Shaw does not introduce other terms that might qualify his paradoxes, that might offer a lever for an audience to pick up and use against the problems presented. The remove of the audience may imply his hope for our critical distance, but more likely he does not want our intrusion. The paradox claims to have a utilitarian function as a critical tool, but in its way it keeps us as much on the surface as the humors of Jonson or the wit of Wycherley. Like their dystopian comedies, the Shavian is totalitarian and exclusionary. It shows us contradictions, certainly, but it closes the boundaries of the world in the name of an all-encompassing unity. When there are neither villains nor heroes, there is no room for the censure of ridicule: all is forgiveness and we are not too far from the sentimental realm of a kindly Providence. While this vision appears to be inclusive, it finally offers only the completed perception of Shaw himself and does not include the audience. Shakespeare's inclusiveness is also forgiving and suggests a paradoxical relation between virtue and vice, but Shakespeare offers that paradox to the audience with a "what you will" attitude and with no sense that he expects to change human nature or reform society. Shakespeare does not suggest that there are neither villains nor heroes: he accepts the moral distinction and then finds a structure that includes both. In refusing the moral distinction, Shaw presumes the status of the maker of a divine comedy, but in his comedy there is neither degree nor proportion: all is dialectic. Like Shakespeare, Shaw escapes to the fantastic and the nonrealistic, but he does so with no sense of the psychic solace that Shakespeare's fantasy offers. Shaw's fantasies—the social utopias—pretend, if not to realism, at least to rationality.

To look ahead to the next chapter, we can see in the work of Tom Stoppard a similar use of paradox, and we find a similar difficulty in identifying the utopian or dystopian vision. The paradox is both disruptive and ideal. Although it usually gives the impression of profundity, it is largely a device of the surface. It is an aesthetic device before it is a moral one. Like a pun, the paradox may or may not have further significance. We inevitably delight in its form, not its content, for it is elegantly absurd. We enjoy being cheated out of easy meanings and having the impossible irrefutably proven. We delight in the absurdity of imagining a social utopia founded a munitions factory as we delight in the *trompe l'oeil* of the famous rabbit and duck that we see simultaneously. The usefulness of the paradox stems from its potential not only for new perceptions but for an awareness of the moment in which perceptions are made. Usefulness and delight overlap in the paradox, but neither takes us deeply into the substance of an issue: the form keeps us at the surface level. Shaw aims his dialectic at the rethinking of society and the sources of its crimes—poverty, war, oppression—and Stoppard aims at the sources of knowledge itself. The differences between them might best be described in terms of grammatical moods: Shaw's paradoxes are consistently in the indicative mood, and the world he creates is likewise indicative, having the appearance of the real and the concrete. Stoppard's paradoxes are in the subjunctive mood: his world is hypothetical, potential, possible, and nonexistent, based on the foundation of an "if." The indicative mood implies that it represents the world as it is no matter how fantastic the representation might be. The subjunctive mood implies a world as it might be, no matter how real it might appear. Because of its indicative nature, Shaw's world seems concrete. In this sense the world is a caricature whose features are reduced to the infinitely evolving paradoxes of Shaw's own mind.

7

Stoppard's Paradox
Delight in Utopia

CECILY: The sole duty and justification for art is social criticism.

CARR: That is a most interesting view of the sole duty and justification for art, Cecily, but it has the disadvantage that a great deal of what we call art has no such function and yet in some way it gratifies a hunger that is common to princes and peasants.

Travesties

When Malvolio interrupts the raucous singing and dancing of Sir Toby Belch in *Twelfth Night*, he asks, "Is there no respect of place, persons nor time in you?" Toby and Feste continue their singing and Toby finally replies, "Dost thou think because thou art virtuous there shall be no more cakes and ale?" Our delight in the scene comes in part from Toby's irrepressibility as he continues his capering in spite of Malvolio's restrictive presence. The principle of this delight is at the heart of comedy, which ruptures the confining bonds of moral authoritarianism with the irrepressible action of revelry and thumbs the nose at imposed limitations, delighting in the body's natural appetites for food, drink, and fun. Toby and Malvolio enact both the aesthetic and the moral debate between order and chaos, virtue and appetite: they take positions in that debate and to some extent serve as agents of the principles, but in the concrete instance they show (as characters) no awareness of their function. It is up to the interpreters of the play to see the characters' roles as structural elements of a thematic concern.

Cecily and Carr, in the passage from Stoppard's *Travesties* that is the epigraph of this chapter, are debating almost exactly the same issue in its modern guise.[1] This debate, too, is both aesthetic and moral; it concerns the question not only of form and formlessness but also of the moral and social responsibility of art. For modern times, virtue equals social criticism and political responsibility. Cecily argues the Marxist's position that all human acts are political; that art must serve society by changing society; and that art satisfies princes and peasants only as it either affirms or offers consolation for the existing social and economic structures that divided princes and peasants in the first place. Cecily's position, like Malvolio's, is clearly moral, but also like Malvolio's it imposes a limitation that does not fully account for the appetitive human nature that seeks delight for its own sake. As Carr suggests, the appetite for art persists regardless of morality, and is satisfied in spite of any social irresponsibility. The dictates of political conscience to correct and improve society do not necessarily lead to the creation of art. The appetite for revelry and delight and for formlessness (as when Tristan Tzara takes scissors to Shakespeare's sonnet or when James Joyce ruptures the traditional form of the novel) that leads to new forms generates the means of satisfaction despite the best intentions of moralists like Malvolio or social realists like Cecily, who speaks here as Lenin's amanuensis. The creation of new forms of art will persist like cakes and ale. Only further evaluation and interpretation will decide whether those forms are good or bad.

In Shakespeare, appetite has various forms and manifestations: for food, for drink, for love, for virtue. It creates a thematic coherence of particular characters and incidents in a schematic whole, yet we delight in the particularity of character and incident in which the theme resides. In Stoppard, there is even less distinction between theme and character because the generality of theme and the particularity of character are so utterly entwined as to be indistinguishable. Stoppard's characters differ from the "naturalistic" characters of

1. Tom Stoppard, *Travesties* (New York: Grove Press, 1975), p. 74. Subsequent citations from the play will be given parenthetically in the text.

sentimental comedy in lacking a hidden emotional or psychic depth: in the naturalistic character what is "real" is what is hidden. Stoppard may leave much unspoken, but like his themes, his characters are in constant view and their concerns are identical to those of the play. When Carr and Cecily argue over the social responsibility of art, they argue as characters, to be sure, but they also present the manifest content of the play. Stoppard's characters, like Shaw's, do not speak like rounded, naturalistic characters. They are more at the mercy of ideas than of circumstances, or at the very least, circumstances are the immediate consequences of thought. We can look directly at the speeches of the characters to understand the playwright's concern.

The themes of social responsibility and art as an indulgence are nicely encapsulated in the exchange between Carr and Cecily quoted in the chapter epigraph. The exchange is especially funny, however, because it is also a conventional lovers' quarrel, so that it is impossible to know whether the argument is heated by the passion of ideas or the passion of lust. Shaw would probably continue the discussion until he somehow proved that Victorian high comedy is socially responsible and corrective—to the point, that is, of a perverse irony. Stoppard does something entirely different and is able to keep both the ideas and the passion on the surface. He resists making a statement, even a perverse or ironic one, yet the ironies are manifold. In *Major Barbara*, Shaw takes us to an ironic proof that the "way of life is through the factory of death." At the same time, he seems to indicate a metaphysical truth behind his irony. It is partially this indicating that distinguishes Shaw from Stoppard. In the previous chapter, I used the terms *indicative* and *subjunctive* to suggest the distinction. Stoppard keeps all his ironies moving, as though he were juggling ideas. He never lets them rest in the indicative mood, never, at least in *Travesties*, lets them point at what they mean, for his meaning is in the act of "juggling" itself. In this play especially, the action is hypothetical and at a remove. Not even an idea of "creative evolution" is held in reserve as a larger truth behind the action. The subjunctive mood removes the play from the ground of represented reality and puts it into the field of play of the mind.

The convolutions of that field of play are enormously complicated in *Travesties*. Carr, for example, is in love with Cecily but is being forced to play out a disguise as Tristan Tzara. The real Tzara created this ruse in a replica of the Jack/Algernon confusion in *The Importance of Being Earnest* to gain Cecily's approval for himself. Cecily is defending the real Tzara, whom she believes is Carr's brother Jack. She accuses Carr of discussing the problem of art only as a tactic, when he is really trying to imagine her "stripped off to her knickers," at which point the lights go down, "coloured lights begin to play over her body," and "comes the sound of the big band playing 'The Stripper'" (p. 78) while Cecily goes on to give statistics on economic oppression in England. Here we return to the overarching theme that subsumes even the debate over indulgence and responsibility or at least defines that debate in larger terms: that the scene and the play itself are functions of Carr's imagination. Stoppard tells us throughout that the play is a reconstruction, and a faulty one at that. The theme, in other words, is perfectly clear and simple. But if Shaw kept to such a simplicity, he would still indicate the theme in the form of a rational paradox. Stoppard complicates and elaborates on the theme by eliminating its symmetry, by bringing fiction, history, memory, literature, and criticism onto a collision course that explodes in a travesty of reality.

One can scarcely untangle the threads of *Travesties* without a tedious rehearsal of the play. Stoppard begins with an apparently minor premise: that Henry Carr, James Joyce, Tristan Tzara, and Lenin *might* have met in Zurich in 1917–1918 and that they *might* have been connected by a production of *The Importance of Being Earnest*, as historically Henry Carr and Joyce were. One could be literal about this premise and try to imagine the conversations the four men might have had. But Stoppard does not presume that one could present such conversations as real; the problem of imagining the meeting is his premise. His own necessarily faulty reconstruction of such an imaginary event is reflected by his Henry Carr, whom we see trying to reproduce the meetings from memory. The result is a partial construction of imagination and memory, of historical fact and fiction. But Carr's construction refers not simply to the historical events (or nonevents) but to Stoppard's own play and to the failure of art ever to reproduce actuality. The premise puts the entire play into the subjunctive mood and makes an issue of reconciling the subjunctive of fiction with the indicative of historical reality.

The historical vignette is precise: one Henry Carr, a minor diplomat in Zurich, performed in *The Importance of Being Earnest* with a group called the English Players. This is remarkable only because James Joyce (who was not yet *the* James Joyce, author of *Ulysses*) was business manager for the group and became embroiled in a lawsuit with Carr over the cost of Carr's trousers, the price of five tickets, and a case of slander. The vignette is funny enough, but only because of the magnitude of Joyce's later achievement compared to the triviality of the incident. It is funny because we have come to perceive Joyce not as an ordinary man who could become involved in mundane and trivial affairs but as one of the great revolutionaries in art. James Joyce, like Shakespeare, has become an idea of a creator, and it is difficult to picture an idea pursuing a lawsuit over the price of five tickets. The vignette itself suits the Stoppardian imagination, an imagination that consistently sees the *idea* of things or people or places in collision with actuality and finds the collision funny. The historical incident is a fitting occasion for that imagination: Stoppard discovers an actual absurdity and makes it, by a logical and imaginative extension, even more absurd.

The scene of Zurich in 1917–1918 is also put to a Stoppardian use. It is a combined location that connects the actual with the imaginary. Uninterested in the particularities of its geography, Stoppard uses it for the very idea of particularity in a historical moment. As a scene it is as much temporal as local, because it is at the nexus of actuality and the perceiving mind. This Zurich in 1917–1918 is not a symbolic place. It is more like an event than a locale because it is a place that happens in Carr's memory—a place created in the mind and only tenuously connected to an actual Zurich. Stoppard's Zurich exists in the gap between the actual and the perceived and perfectly reflects the gaps in Carr's memory ("What a bloody country even the cheese has got holes in it" [p. 29]). The scene manifests a possibility, like the scene of *Rosencrantz and Guildenstern Are Dead*. In that play too an imaginative potential is made actual (if unidentifiable), and the result is a collision of the real and the perceived. *Rosencrantz and Guildenstern* displaces its characters from their natural habitat in *Hamlet*. The scene is a result of an intentional confusion between actor and character. That is, it is customary enough to ask, What happens to an actor when he walks offstage? and to make a play out of the answer to that question. There is a logical (if absurd) corollary in the question, What happens to a character offstage? To what place does a character exit? The answer is the premise of *Rosencrantz and Guildenstern*: to a place "without any visible character," which suspends the laws of probability because it is an improbable place. It is less a waiting room from which to make entrances than a temporal suspension where, every so often, the play catches up to characters. The scene of *Rosencrantz and Guildenstern* is a place of relative motions in collision. Without the momentary meetings with *Hamlet*, Rosencrantz and Guildenstern exist but do not function. They *are*, in an absolute sense, and they are performing for us, to be sure, in a play called *Rosencrantz and Guildenstern Are Dead*, but their dramatic problem as characters is that they are performing without purpose. And to exist in the absolute, without the contingencies and relativity of actuality (which in this case is a further fiction), is to lead an absurd existence, like any Didi or Gogo. This play is circular because it is the very thing that offers Rosencrantz and Guildenstern their meaning and their significance, the very thing that brings with it the laws of probability (because it also brings the law of inevitability: death) but is itself a fiction. The play points at the problem of a created world in relation to actuality, its difficulty in leaping out of itself and bridging the gap to reality.

The Stoppardian scene tends to be an emphatically self-conscious artifice, but the artifice is entirely consistent with comic convention in which the artificiality of the play's scene and action is openly acknowledged. The scene is exempt from the laws of actuality, society, and politics in both *Travesties* and *Rosencrantz and Guildenstern*. Throughout his plays, Stoppard may use specific sites: a library, a room, a professorial study, Zurich in 1917; but these sites are not objective touchstones for the dramatic action, nor are they naturalistic sites in the sense that they represent or symbolically reflect the causality of the action. Most of the sites are familiar, but they often refer to theatrical, not natural, conventions and they recall for us other theaters, other plays. Stoppard deliberately traps his locales in the theater so that they manifest their own status as theatrical sites. Zurich is as much a place "without any visible character" as the vaguely Elizabethan stage of *Rosencrantz and Guildenstern*. The acrobatics of the jumpers through the professor's study in *Jumpers* remind the audience that it is in a performance space. Carr's "Room" can look very much like a drawing room out of *The Importance of Being Earnest*. At the very least, it is designed in the period style of the First World War, not to refer to that period but to remind us of the temporal conflation in the play, where "most of the action takes place within Carr's memory" (p. 17).

One of the paradoxes in Stoppard's fiction is that no matter how far the mind ranges with ideas or potentials or possibilities, it finally returns to the inexplicable concreteness of objective physical reality. The theatrical space is necessarily concrete and objective: every action must be someplace, and there is no escape from the phenomenal presence. Yet in spite of its concreteness, the theatrical space is still the product of imagination, the local habitation of airy nothing. That paradox keeps Stoppard's sites from being substantive. Perhaps Stoppard's living rooms in *The Real Thing* most nearly approximate a substantive site, but even in that play Stoppard insists that the rooms are theatrical fictions. We discover this when we see that the first scene of the play has been taken almost verbatim from the "real" life of the author in the second scene. The significance of each room, in other words, depends on when it appears in the sequence of the narrative. The temporal aspects of a scene are especially clear in *Travesties* when we recognize that Stoppard is trying to create a play that takes place within the site of a memory. The problem is directly analogous to that of creating a play out of imagination. Both memory and imagination necessarily produce a faulty re-creation of the actual world, yet that re-creation is bound by the actualities of time and space in the theatrical site. In *Travesties*, not only are the scenes mobile in almost an Elizabethan sense, but their mobility corresponds to the alternation between past and present, the conflation of imaginary and historical time, and the combination of historical fact and fictional present. The subjective space of Carr's memory, if it makes any reference at all, refers to the subjective space of the "implied author" whose presence is pervasive. The play thus closes in upon itself as a created artifice.

Much of the critical work on Stoppard has explored the philosophical underpinnings and implications of his plays and has helped establish the conceptual context in which they operate. A debate over the philosophical validity of *Jumpers* stirred the pages of *Philosophy*,[2] and Stoppard's use of philosophers from George Moore to Wittgenstein has been thoroughly discussed. Self-referentiality, the Strange Loop, and the Tangled Hierarchy, which can be said to constitute both the structure and the significance of the plays, have put Stoppard deep in the heart of modern aesthetic and conceptual territory.[3] Robert Brustein brought a famous complaint against *Rosencrantz and Guildenstern*, saying that there is "something disturbingly voguish and available about this play, as well as a prevailing strain of cuteness," and that it offers "a form of Beckett without tears."[4] The complaint is that Stoppard writes amusing and available comedies, which he implants with

2. The controversy was carried on between Jonathan Bennett, "Philosophy and Mr. Stoppard," *Philosophy* 50 (1975): 5; and Henning Jensen, "Jonathan Bennett and Mr. Stoppard," *Philosophy* 52 (1977): 215.

3. Though Stoppard is never mentioned, his plays fit the conceptual premises discussed in Douglas R. Hofstadter, *Godel, Escher, Bach: An Eternal Golden Braid* (New York: Random House, Vintage Books, 1979).

4. Robert Brustein, "Waiting for Hamlet," *New Republic* 4 (November 1967): 25.

ideas that imply larger significance; but he does not follow up that significance. The implication is that comedy may be delightful, may avoid social significance, but it ought not to raise philosophical issues in a playful manner; Stoppard ought not to smudge serious ideas with frivolity, cuteness, or university wit. The complaint suggests how readily we look to the conceptual content of a play as the measure of its usefulness, forgetting that content is often the raw material of a form or genre that alters whatever material it receives, whether marriage and cuckoldry, corrupt political institutions, obsessions, young love, or social injustice and hypocrisy. Stoppard takes ideas as his material, but that material serves comic ends first ("What I try to do, is to end up by contriving the perfect marriage between the play of ideas and farce or perhaps even high comedy").[5] When we try to discover the significative effect of ideas in Stoppard, their statement about the world, their use, we neglect their delight, or at least we cannot believe that their use is their delight as comic material.

We want, in other words, to make great significance out of Stoppard's theatrical self-consciousness. But Stoppard turns that very signification to comic delight, exempting the plays from the seriousness of a Beckett. The death of the Player in *Rosencrantz and Guildenstern* sends a potentially serious message: that we can experience death only through its artful imitation, that artifice is the only way to know about death without actually dying.[6] Art is the residue of experience and a travesty of reality, but only through art can we come to know reality. This is the consistent paradox in Stoppard's work. It is not the rational paradox that Shaw demonstrates by proving that contradictory propositions are equally true. It is instead a paradox at the base of artistic creation itself, and it adheres to almost all of Stoppard's work. Even a play like *The Real Thing* that seems to domesticate his comedy in the problems of love

5. Tom Stoppard, "Ambushes for Audiences: Toward a High Comedy of Ideas," interview in *Theatre Quarterly* 4 (May–July 1974): 7.
6. For a development of this idea, see Robert Egan, "The Thin Beam of Light: The Purpose of Playing in *Rosencrantz and Guildenstern Are Dead*," *Theatre Journal* 31 (March 1979): 59.

and marriage points at the process of making art out of experience and at the consequent loss of reality, so that the only experience possible is in the art itself.

Stoppard's scenes are literally "utopian" in that they are no place. They do not duplicate a reality but constitute a reality. Although the premise is that the imaginary world does not escape the real, at least in the theater, in Stoppard this is a subject not for instruction but for delight—and thus Stoppard is a comic, not a philosophical, playwright. To take a play like *Travesties* too far outside its self-contained delight is to misconstrue its comic genre. From one perspective, self-containment and self-referentiality in the structure of the play isolate the artifact from the real world of the audience insofar as they refuse to implicate the work in the social or moral world of that audience. Stoppard, unlike Shaw, does not suggest the reform of reason. But from another perspective, structured artificiality and self-reference place the work in the world with the audience, just as the Vice figure of the comic morality brings the audience into his plan.

To examine this effect, we might look at the cast of characters in *Travesties*. The play is inhabited by historical personalities, Lenin, Joyce, and Tristan Tzara; by fictional derivatives, Gwendolyn, Cecily, and Bennett; and by one unknown but historical derivative, Henry Carr. Each character comes from a distinct level of actuality: historical, fictional, or mundane. The play equalizes these levels by giving all the characters the same ontological status in the comedy, and at the same time it uses the audience's awareness of the differences as a source of its comic premise. The conflation of the historical and the fictional elements makes the play less probable on the one hand but more real on the other. The cast of characters is a Tangled Hierarchy of the actual and the fictional, and the tangle includes the audience's awareness and perception of historical and fictional precedents. This cast bridges the gaps between audience and play and world and says that the play is simultaneously an artifice and an actuality. Stoppard uses the fact that any fiction is neither completely in the world nor completely apart from it and makes visible the fact that fiction's ontological status is an element of our delight. The audience is thus brought into the play much as it would be if a Vice character came forward and said, This is a play and this is what I am going to create for you. In fact, one of the characters in *Travesties* does exactly that. Henry Carr comes out after the first library scene with a narrative recollection of life in Zurich with Joyce, Lenin, and Tzara. But in his long monologue it is clear that we are getting not the truth but the faulty and prejudiced memory of an imaginary past. The narrative style of Carr's monologue suggests that we ought to be getting the truth, for narrative is the style of omniscience. But instead of omniscience we get the outburst of prejudice that derives from the mundane (and actual) conflict of Carr and Joyce, an imperfect knowledge of Lenin and what Carr titles *Memoirs of Dada by a Consular Friend of the Famous in Old Zurich*.[7]

If Shaw had imagined the collision of the characters in *Travesties*, he might well have let them debate the substantive issues of art, politics, and revolution. And indeed some of the long speeches in the play have the quality of Shavian arias that burst out in an exuberant rhetorical revel and give us pleasure in the energy, wit, and style of language itself. But the debates in Stoppard exceed the rational content in a way different from that in which Shaw's musicality exceeds his content. In *Travesties*, at least, a concrete use of literary styles rather than musicality brings the aesthetic dimension to the language.

---

7. The coda of Carr's speech is a recollection of Joyce (*Travesties*, pp. 22–23): "A prudish, prudent man, Joyce, in no way profligate or vulgar, and yet convivial, without being spend-thrift, and yet still without primness towards hard currency in all its transmutable and transferable forms and denominations, of which, however, he demanded only a sufficiency from the world at large, exhibiting a monkish unconcern for worldly and bodily comforts, without at the same time shutting himself off from the richness of human society, whose temptations, on the other hand, he met with an ascetic disregard tempered only by sudden and catastrophic aberrations—in short, a complex personality, an enigma, a contradictory spokesman for the truth, an obsessive litigant and yet an essentially private man who wished his total indifference to public notice to be universally recognized—in short a liar and a hypocrite, a tight-fisted, sponging, fornicating drunk not worth the paper, that's that bit done."

Stoppard structures his play through the collision of styles as much as through the collision of characters, for to a large extent style and character are identical. *Travesties* is a litany of styles: the limericks and the narrative stream of consciousness of Joyce as well as form of liturgical responsion in Joyce's dialogue, the epigrams of Oscar Wilde, the broken and interrupted sequences of Dada poetry (using on one occasion Shakespeare's eighteenth sonnet, "Shall I compare thee to a summer's day"), historical narrative from the memos of the British consulate, the political discourse of Lenin, the patter of the music hall (specifically the rhythms of "Mr. Gallagher and Mr. Shean"). The collision of styles creates what Stoppard himself has called the "architecture" of the play.[8]

The architecture of conflicting styles creates an unusually clear unity of form and content. *Travesties* is built on the travesties of other literary and dramatic arts as much as those arts are built on a travesty of actuality. Other literary forms and styles are as much the premise of *Travesties* as *Hamlet* is the premise of *Rosencrantz and Guildenstern*, or detective fiction of *The Real Inspector Hound*, or surrealism of *After Magritte*, or Wittgenstein of *Dogg's Hamlet*. The consistent foundation of Stoppard's art is other art. From one perspective, style is rootless; it is the pure manipulation of form. From another, style is all there is; it is the necessary and unavoidable construction of reality in the only way it can be known; art, literary art in particular, is trapped in the tradition of styles as the available means of knowing. Stoppard's paradox thus lies in epistemol-

---

8. Stoppard, quoted in Ronald Hayman, *Tom Stoppard* (London: Heinemann, 1978), p. 10. The full quotation reveals Stoppard's awareness of the dichotomy between use and delight in comedy: "What I was trying was this. What I'm always trying to say is 'Firstly A. Secondly, minus A.' What was supposed to be happening was that we have this rather frivolous nonsense going on, and then the Lenin section comes in and says, 'Life is too important. We can't afford this artificial frivolity, this nonsense going on in the arts.' Then he says, 'Right. That's what I've got to say,' and he sits down. Then the play stands up and says, 'You thought *that* was frivolous? You ain't seen nothing yet.' And you go into the Gallagher and Shean routine. That was the architectural thing I was after."

ogy: what we know is defined by our style, that is, our manner of knowing.[9] The further moral problem in this premise is then the degree to which we are responsible, or art is responsible, for changing the world. For the effort to change presumes a knowledge of what, in fact, would be a better world, what revolution in art or politics would indeed bring improved conditions. Yet the very idea of improvement demands some rooted sense of what constitutes the Good. Lenin, presumably, knows. His linguistic style of political discourse that enumerates statistical proofs of evil in the world's societies suggests not only that knowledge of the Good is possible but also that art can serve that knowledge. The result of such a premise is the extreme utilitarianism of Soviet realism, which is the political version of a morality play. In the architecture of Stoppard's play, however, Lenin's style (and political position) is just one among several and is in a dialectical relation with the style of the purest aesthetician of all, Oscar Wilde. This dialectic, one of Stoppard's jokes, consists of style as much as matter. The play itself disrupts any simple two-sided dialectic, however, with its melange of styles, so that rather than a symmetrical paradox or contradiction, the voices create an endless chain of qualification: not "either/or" but "this and this and . . ."

Stoppard's specifically theatrical use of his material partly qualifies the dialectic. By this I mean that Stoppard makes jokes not only for the audience but on the audience as well, on all of us who insist on looking for the significative content or the social, political, or moral message that validates our concern for usefulness. "Cecily's Lecture" at the beginning of act 2 is just such a joke on usefulness. Cecily waits for the returning audience to be seated, then begins a long lecture on the history of the revolution, the economic theory of Marx, and the progress of Lenin toward Russia. The irony of the

9. See two versions of this idea in E. H. Gombrich, *Art and Illusion: A Study in the Psychology of Pictorial Representation*, Bollingen Series (Princeton, N.J.: Princeton University Press, 1960); and Nelson Goodman, *Ways of Worldmaking* (Hassocks, England: Harvester Press, 1978).

speech can easily be missed because of its theatrical tedium, and Stoppard allows for cutting it. But he has also explained it:

> There are several levels going on here, and one of them is that what I personally like is the theatre of audacity. I thought, "Right. We'll have a rollicking first act, and they'll all come back from their gin-and-tonics thinking "isn't it fun? What a lot of lovely jokes!" And they'll sit down, and this pretty girl will start talking about the theory of Marxism and the theory of capitalism and the theory of value. And the smiles, because they're not prepared for it, will atrophy." And that to me was a joke in itself.[10]

Stoppard is playing with the audience's own expectations of use and delight, but the joke is on the audience. If it is set up for a frivolous romp, it will not look for social significance, just as when it is set up for significance, it may be offended by jokes. The intrusion of Cecily's lecture is audacious because it is dangerously tedious in the theater. It also says to the audience, "If you want social reform in the theater, here is the real thing," and we realize that the style of political and social reform is not wholly appropriate to the style of theatrical delight and that it is probably impossible to accommodate political acts to artistic forms. The style of the political speech is one among many styles parodied in the play, but it stands in isolation; it cannot be wholly incorporated, yet it is a crucial dimension of the arena in which usefulness debates delight.

When Stoppard talks about his own view of politically relevant art, he recalls W. H. Auden's saying that his poems never saved a single Jew from the gas chamber and says that if one wants immediate action on a particular injustice or immorality, then the worst thing to do is write a play.[11] Not only is that ineffective, he says, but it also creates "bad art." The *Theatre Quarterly* interviewer asks Stoppard whether philosophical and political neutrality is not simply a hopeless despair over the efficacy of any play. Stoppard replies by trying

---

10. Stoppard, quoted in Hayman, *Tom Stoppard*, p. 9.
11. Stoppard, "Ambushes for Audiences," p. 14.

to define the difference between short-term and long-term effectiveness, comparing a newspaper journalist, Adam Raphael, with the playwright Athol Fugard. He notes that after a news piece by Raphael on wages in South Africa, wages went up within forty-eight hours. He goes on to use a significant phrase that defines the difference between immediate political efficacy and the long-term effect of art on culture and sensibility: "Art—Auden or Fugard or the entire cauldron—is important because it provides the moral matrix, the moral sensibility, from which we make our judgements about the world."[12]

Although "moral matrix" may be a somewhat hazy phrase, Stoppard is claiming the right of art to appeal to universals. This claim does not equate universal with absolute, nor does it necessarily suggest the neoclassic idea that art must be grounded in the principles of verisimilitude. Those principles rely on the certainty that one dimension of experience is fixed, changeless, and eternal. Stoppard's principle is uncertainty. This uncertainty does not eliminate the possibility or even the necessity of moral and ethical responsibilities, but Stoppard turns those responsibilities into material for aesthetic, stylistic, and comic manipulation.

The duty of the artist, then, is not necessarily social criticism but the feeding of a hunger for form. The artist stylizes reality and in his style presents his knowledge. Henry Carr tells Tristan Tzara: "To be an artist *at all* is like living in Switzerland during a world war. To be an artist *in Zurich, in 1917,* implies a degree of self-absorption that would have glazed over the eyes of Narcissus" (p. 38). The problem, morally, is not that the artist exempts himself from political consequence and social reality in a perverse "bourgeois-intellectual individualism" but that art itself has a tenuous connection with concrete reality. Art is a neutral territory, unlike politics or religion, because it has no necessary consequences in the real world. Art, like Switzerland, is a created context in, but not necessarily engaged in, the world's wars. It is not necessarily

12. Ibid., p. 16.

a willful perversity that keeps the artist disengaged, Stoppard suggests; it is that art forms, especially literary art forms, are at best patchworks of limited perceptions, faulty memories, and imagined possibilities. On the other hand, art can be made to serve as social or moral criticism, can be didactic, and this function cannot be ignored. But as Carr's speech quoted in the epigraph of this chapter suggests, didacticism and social criticism do not fill the appetite for new forms, for delight, for revolution and change.

Stoppard's comic paradox forms at the juncture of phenomena and the perceiving mind where subjective perception meets an objective reality—a reality that itself may be only hypothetical. This paradox says something about comedy and at least one of its possibilities. Taking Stoppard as an extreme example, in other words, the paradox suggests that part of the function of comedy is epistemological or, to put it another way, that comedy presents the problem of knowledge in the sense that one of its functions is to raise doubt. I do not mean that comedy is simply a form of skepticism but that it ruptures certainties by demonstrating that certainty is the most improbable thing of all. To take the most rudimentary example, we might say that the slip on the banana peel ruptures the certainty that a simple walk can continue indefinitely. The obstacle raises doubt, quite apart from laughter. There is a structural similarity, furthermore, between the potentially infinite momentum of the walker and, say, the assumption that marriage is forever, or that the sole duty and function of art is social criticism. Infinite momentum and infinite moral or social commitment are theoretical possibilities, and the latter might even be considered desirable possibilities. But comedy disrupts mechanistic principles and reminds us of "men as they are" because it brings unlooked-for possibilities and the principle of probability. Comic probability breaks up the momentum of the walker with an obstacle, and even if the banana peel is not a necessary obstacle, or even a probable one, it presents the likelihood of *some* obstacle. If one is certain that the sole duty and function of art is social criticism, the comic argument offers several other possible functions as refutation. It is not necessarily the substance of that refutation that delights us but the fact of the refutation, the intrusion of an alternative. Perhaps the greater the disparity between the nature of the momentum and the nature of the obstacle, the more we delight in their collision. When Carr launches into his refutation of Cecily's "social criticism" argument, the dialogue quickly degenerates to expletives:

CARR: Kindly do not confuse a Dada raffle with Victorian high comedy—
CECILY: Both bourgeois—both decadent—
CARR: You are familiar with neither—
CECILY: Art is a critique of society or it is nothing!
CARR: Do you know Gilbert and Sullivan??!
CECILY: I know Gilbert but not Sullivan.
CARR: Well, if you knew Iolanthe like I know Iolanthe—
CECILY: I doubt it—
CARR: Patience!
CECILY: How dare you!
CARR: Pirates! Pinafore!
CECILY: Control yourself!
CARR: *Ruddigore!*
CECILY: This is a Public Library, Mr. Tzara!
CARR: *GONDOLIERS, Madam!*

(pp. 74-75)

This exchange is funny because it passes from the theoretical premise through the emotional heat to a climax of the concrete ("a Public Library"). The "refutation" is not substantive but stylistic; that is, it is not a simple dialectic or even a rational paradox that Shaw might use to prove an opposite principle. Styles, in other words, have no opposites, they merely have varieties, just as "banana peel" is not the opposite of "walk."

The stylistic variety in *Travesties* thus presents a point about subjectivity in tension with objects. In the Stoppardian perspective, the world of objective phenomena corresponds to theoretical certainties in that claiming certainty of knowledge or morals or reality is akin to claiming that because a person is walking he will walk ad infinitum. The claim to know is like the claim for an infinite present. Somehow change must be accounted for, but change subverts both categorical and theoretical knowledge and the present. On the other hand, of course, there is always and only a present. Stoppard's effort to reconcile the irreconcilable creates his humor, and the tension between the theoretical and the actual becomes an infinite loop, so that often what is "actual" is seen theoretically, and the theoretical is viewed through actuality. In *Jumpers*, for example, Professor George Moore says, "I will now demonstrate that though an arrow is always approaching its target, it never quite gets there, and Saint Sebastian died of fright."[13] George's rabbit, Thumper, alas, dies of this paradox just before the end of the play. Comedy is a free zone where irreconcilable differences can coexist.

One difference between Shaw's and Stoppard's use of paradox is that Shaw's dialectic always seems aimed toward an improvement of reason; he lectures the audience with the sense that "there must be some truth under all this irony." Although his plays never arrive at a truth outside themselves and become aesthetically whole without actually reaching a concrete moral conclusion, still in most of Shaw's plays something seems to have been left out; Shaw seems to withhold a conclusion on purpose, seems, in fact, to have more to say or do. The Shavian play is Hegelian in that the conclusions often seem more like beginnings than endings, as when Cusins promises to be at the munitions factory, or Vivie Warren decides to continue her work with Honoria Fraser, or Tanner continues talking. The arbitrariness in the endings of these plays is not illogical, but the endings are just resting places in a continuing logic and hence have none of the release of more conventional comic resolutions, such as the ritual marriage dance or the entrance of the law. One of our dissatisfactions with Shaw is that he often seems to want to tell us more and that he cannot let his comedies go free. Our discomfort has less to do with a difficult moral posture than with our feeling that the plays have simply stopped. We have been denied both a concrete moral conclusion and a comic artificiality. Although the musicality of his rhetoric transcends the rational

13. Tom Stoppard, *Jumpers* (New York: Grove Press, 1972), p. 28.

arguments and the flights into fantasy betray an idealism or a desire for utopia, Shaw does not escape the style of the preacher, and we are left asking what he is "getting at." Although Shaw's comedies lack concrete utility, they have a utilitarian impulse and convey the dystopian belief that the world is full of error. Stoppard, on the other hand, seems to try to include as much as possible and to avoid the style of the preacher, unless he includes it as one more style in the parade of styles. When his plays turn in on themselves, they are released into the world as comic artifice, with no suggestion that the world he presents ought to be any better than it is. Error is certainly part of that world, but that error is built into the structures of perception or into human nature. The plays themselves are utopian, not in projecting a perfect image of a perfect world but in existing self-consciously as art, which is the only genuinely "perfect" territory in the world.

The utopian comedy I am trying to define does not necessarily represent an ideal but rather presents an object that is self-contained, whereas the dystopian comedy points to its further significative purposes. Dystopian comedies ask us to recognize moral dysfunctions in the plays as moral dysfunctions from the world; utopian comedies encompass both dysfunctions and ideals within the artifact. And the ideal that Stoppard encompasses is the privilege of the art-making process itself. His moral universe is a universe of style. In *Travesties* he echoes Oscar Wilde, the paragon of stylists: "Far from being a bugbear of the Home Rule sodality, Cecily, Wilde was indifferent to politics. He may occasionally have been a little overdressed but he made up for it by being immensely uncommitted" (p. 74).

This quotation is fully packed with allusion in both matter and style. It not only pays homage to Oscar Wilde, who is the literary source of *Travesties*, but also calls up Wilde's homosexuality, the Irish question, the aesthetic premise of art for art's sake, and Wilde's habits of dress (these recur in Henry Carr's obsession for matching trousers); most particularly, it lifts Wilde's epigrammatic style directly from *The Importance of Being Earnest* with a minor but crucial alteration. There is not necessarily buggery in bugbears nor sodomy in sodality, but sounds can become independent of meaning and can exchange meanings through such similarities in sound. Stoppard takes full advantage of the potential for exchange. More than an echo here, style is a palpable presence, a corporeality.[14] The corporeality allows for the structuring of words according to weight, distribution, and balance. Sense is dispersed through the forms of sound. In Wilde's original epigram, Algernon says, "If I am occasionally a little overdressed, I make up for it by being always immensely overeducated." The balance comes from the repetition of "over," suggesting an equality, and from the compensation of "always immensely" for "occasionally a little." The quality of the sound suggests significance, as though overdressed and overeducated were indeed equal and compensating conditions. The formal balance is perfect, but the idea is nonsense, and the humor comes from the collision between sound and sense in the formal purity of the epigram. Stoppard's alteration suggests the same nonsense because it lifts the epigram virtually wholesale from Wilde. It, too, is balanced by the fulcrum of compensation, but the compensatory conditions are no longer equal but opposite ("overdressed" and "uncommitted"). The further difference is that Stoppard's epigram is not really nonsense, for it establishes the conditions of his play, the issues of art for art's sake and political commitment, artistic freedom and political relevance. Further, however, it establishes the roots of the play in another play. It is referential, but its reference is to other art, thus suggesting a significative projection not to the world of actuality but to the world of art and completing the self-referential circle of art as an enclosed and neutral territory.

14. Sigurd Burckhardt, *Shakespearean Meanings* (Princeton, N.J.: Princeton University Press, 1968), pp. 24–25: "The pun is one, I would say the second most primitive way of divesting a word of its meaning. . . . It is the creation of a semantic identity between words whose phonetic identity is, for ordinary language, the merest coincidence. That is to say, it is an act of verbal violence, designed to tear the close bond between a word and its meaning. It asserts that mere phonetic—i.e., material, corporeal—likeness establishes likeness of meaning."

Whatever aesthetic and comic delight, whatever corporeality in language the dystopian comedy may employ, it projects its intentions and implications out from the play toward significance. It may never reveal its ideals, but it implies ideals as either a priori assumptions or goals. The world within the play is comic primarily because it shows us a fallen society. The dystopias of Jonson are often corrected by a judicial imposition; Shaw leaps out of his dystopias to a fantasy in which "there is no wicked side: life is all one," a fantasy that despite its inclusiveness falls short because it is also too far ahead of the play. The Restoration comedy brings its dystopia to so perfect an inversion that the extremity of its "fallen" world is itself an aesthetic perfection, and it lies on the razor's edge between a negative signification and a positive aesthetic assertion. Whenever the elements of delight come to the surface, they lead the play and the audience toward the utopian perspective, for the utopian and the delightful, like the dystopian and the utilitarian, are natural bedfellows. The latter two lead out from the artifact and the former two are wholly contained within it. Shaw would be a utopian playwright but for his inability to give over his comedies to themselves and their artifice. Stoppard not only gives over his plays to their own artificiality and style but also gives them to the idea of artifice itself. He does not try to prove, as Shaw does, that "life is all one," because the plays do not take the form of a proof. To put it another way, if Shaw's plays tend to conclude with the imaginary or the fantastic, Stoppard's begin with an imaginary premise. The indicative mood suits the dystopian perspective; the subjunctive mood suits utopias. The premise "what if" introduces possibilities and potentials whereas the premise "it is" indicates a world already out of joint.

Stoppard is a utopian playwright not because he avoids specific political or social material; he does not avoid it. What could be more specific than speeches lifted directly from Lenin's own texts? That specific material, however, becomes part of a larger perspective that takes in phenomena at the same level of ignorance, on the principle that multiple perspectives rupture the unity of a single phenomenon. The principles of subjectivity necessarily invade the integrity of the objective world. In the aesthetic of painting, this principle works as a deliberate confusion of figure and ground, so that the two cannot be distinguished. Some modern art, for example, eliminates the single vanishing point of perspective by which a viewer can distinguish foreground and background and replaces it with subjective perspectives. In *Artist Descending a Staircase*, Stoppard uses the principle in a concrete situation. The character Sophie knows only that she loves the artist who painted a "snow scene"—a painting of a field of snow with black lines on it. At the end of the play, two other characters discover that she loved the wrong man—that the painting she described was conceived by the artist as a white fence with black gaps between the posts. The point is not simply that Stoppard applies a theoretical or aesthetic premise to a concrete human situation but that his own aesthetic principle is deliberately to confuse figure and ground so that we cannot separate characters from their ideas, ideas from dramatic structure, or structure from delight. Stoppard's new kind of universal principle insists on the multiplicity of subjectivity rather than the unity of objectivity, and his method is to bring all his aesthetic elements to the same ontological plane of fiction.

Stoppard's inclusiveness in his utopian method incorporates the unknown as a necessary adjunct of subjectivity. But this inclusiveness is also part of the comic principle that presumes there will always be "something else." Whether one calls this something else the element of the probable, of everyday life, of things as they are, of the life force, of renewal, or of regeneration, the principle is the same. Carr's concluding speech in *Travesties* is a case in point. "I learned three things in Zurich during the war. I wrote them down. Firstly, you're either a revolutionary or you're not, and if you're not you might as well be an artist as anything else. Secondly, if you can't be an artist, you might as well be a revolutionary. . . . I forget the third thing" (pp. 98–99). This is funny partly because Henry has become a dotty old man. But it also gets directly to the heart of our delight and satisfaction in comedy when we expect something further that is unknown or forgotten. In some sense comedy is the genre of the excluded middle, of what persists outside the symmetry of dialectics, the rationality of syllogisms, the certainty of moral premises. The "third thing" may be disastrous—it may be a banana peel or a revolution—but it is delightful and hopeful because it suggests there is more to come; it is probable, if not inevitable; it is the unknown that lurks in the wings or in the imagination of a playwright, and we anticipate it with a delighted, apprehensive tremor; it is the comic version of the "reality" principle that there will always be something else that brings change and continuance and that our art forms are only temporary closures on experience.

8

Forms of Delight

But that's all one, our play is done,
And we'll strive to please you every day.
Twelfth Night

The notion that comedy is the genre of "men as they are" is remarkably enduring. In various formulations, comedy is the genre of the actual rather than the ideal, the social rather than the individual, the biological rather than the spiritual. If we take the basic notion not as a proscriptive definition or classifying category but as an extreme compression of complex social and aesthetic factors, we might decompress the idea to discover not what comedy is but how it functions.

In the first place, there are political implications in the idea that comedy reflects humans in their social groupings, habits, manners, and ethics. One aspect of the usefulness of comedy is indeed its reflection of an immediate social condition. The social element of comic concerns is suggested as early as Aristotle's assertion that comedy began in a lampooning mode of revelry and derision and is continued in Bergson's assertion that laughter itself is a social corrective that breaks through the rigidity of habit. Insofar as it imitates, comedy is indeed the mirror of manners. A further political implication, however, comes from the subversive potential of laughter and revelry and comic misrule: as the truly social genre, comedy threatens and even assaults the structures of authority and oppression. But the danger in stressing either of these political implications is that we might then look only for the instrumental force, or "message," of the comedy. We can find that force in satire, but if we look only for social and political efficacy, most comedies leave a great deal wanting.

One further implication of the political nature of comedy is what its social nature suggests about the relation of any given work or performance to its audience. Beyond either corrective or cathartic uses, comedy creates a social relation between fiction and reality. We might say that the aesthetic or delightful elements of comedy have little to do with imitation or with policy and much to do with comedy's presence in and of the "polis." As comedy is impelled by the mock attack on structures of the community, so comic forms reach out into the audience; the fictive assaults the real. The actual invective may be long gone, but more than other genres, comedy needs the reciprocity between the work and the world that demands the sharing of time and space in a historical moment: it demands the aesthetic of "presence" in the fullest sense. If we use temporal terms for such presence we could say that at its extremes comedy stretches from the moment of performance that lacks duration, which we could call delight, to enduring meaning, order, and form, which we could call use. In practice, of course, delight and use are great equivocators. All kinds of performances require the actual or implicit presence of an audience. When we find a display of actor over character, of skill and virtuosity over content, we are at an extremity of comic delight. The most radical instance of such extremity is the moment when an actor breaks up and "infects" the audience with his laughter. We may not know why, but we generally join in. What distinguishes the performatory sharing at this extreme is that the invitation to participate must come from the stage or performer to the audience. The resulting laughter is not that of an audience laughing at a mistake. It occurs when the fictional world claims the relevance of immediacy by an emphatic recognition of the ephemeral pleasure in the unity of actor and audience joined in laughter. The further a play removes itself from the immediacy of the audience—as it emphasizes character over actor, narrative or theme over performance—the more it establishes itself with the durable features of form and usefulness.

This distinction between the ephemeral and the durable features of comedy is perhaps best illustrated in comic characters. At the performative extreme is the clown, who exists only during his performance and whose being is pure spectacle. At the other extreme is the dramatic character who endures because of his connection to the narrative line of the drama. Such a character is formed and completed by the development of the plot,[1] unlike the clown, who is continually improvising his existence. In actual performance, of course, the two extremes commingle, and the clown's performance may find a narrative shape as much as the dramatic character may appear spontaneous. A further distinction, however, may be made on the basis of how characters display moral features: whether the behavior of a character identifies its whole moral construction (as in Jonson's humored characters) or is symptomatic of a hidden moral and emotional interior. The difference between Horner in *The Country Wife* and Bevil in *The Conscious Lovers* can illustrate this distinction.

Whereas Horner's display of wit is a "spectacle" of character, Bevil's demonstration of feeling and benevolence is a proof of interiority. It is Bevil, not Horner, who is the distant progenitor of the naturalistic characters of realism. In the Aristotelian terms with which Bert States defines this range in dramatic character, from *ethos* to *opsis*,[2] we might also compare the characters of Jonson and Shakespeare. Jonson's humored characters display their ethical features as masks: moral character is identical to feature. Moreover, the structure of Jonson's plot is "performatory" in the sense that it tends to repeat versions of the moral problem in serial form, like the improvisations of the clown as opposed to the development and gain in Shakespeare's comic plots. Shakespeare's characters

1. See Bert O. States, "The Anatomy of Dramatic Character," *Theatre Journal* 37, no. 1 (March 1985): 88. "Thus the cathartic psychology behind the ending of a play is the arrival of a perfect tautology between existence and personal nature as seen in the interplay of their dramatic analogues, plot and character."

2. Ibid., p. 93. "One might say that the affective power of dramatic character runs on an axis from *ethos* to *opsis*, from moral code to personal manner, or (in Horatian terms) from the useful (*utile*) to the delightful (*dulce*). What plays allow us to see, then, is an intensification of the inside and outside of the human being, our moral and mannerly possibilities carried to extremes."

generally suggest an ethical interior and appear to make complex choices based on a variety of motives and reasons. As a
result, these characters appear more enduring than Jonson's
and seem less in need of performance for their existence. We
can contemplate Malvolio in a way that we need not contemplate Sir Epicure Mammon.

Tragic characters tend to be ethically individuated and to
move further and further into isolation from social circumstances. The sense of individuation gives such characters their
quality of "likelihood" as well as their duration. Comic characters are generally less "likely," especially as they lean toward the performance mode and to the generality of the comic
"type" that reduces character to a single moral drive. The
more individuated a comic character is—the greater the interiority and the more complex the ethical choices available to
that character—the more "useful" that character is in terms of
duration. On the other hand, the more a character is reduced
to external and minimal moral features, the more efficient that
character is as a moral comment in immediate circumstances.
This need for reductive efficiency would certainly account for
the habitual use in political satire of the cartoonlike elements
of human character: it is matter of immediate efficacy in performance, not of the slow, complex discovery of thought over
time.

The tragic plot tends to take us through the process of individuation. A tragic hero likewise sums up the tragic "moment" in his fictional experience and is the center and source
of the experience. Comedy tends to engage us more by events
and plot than by individual characters. By this I mean we are
in fact less concerned to see what a comic character will become or how he or she will "turn out" because a comic character is generally as fully realized at the beginning of a play as
at the end. What changes in comedy is not character but circumstance. We are interested to see what will happen but
probably more interested to see how it happens. In comedy,
that is, we tend to demand and expect the display of virtuosity, skill, and performance by the playwright in the structure
of the plot. The appeal of the comic plot is not only its end but

the dexterity, surprise, and cleverness of the means to that end.[3]

Comedy leads toward a social event that suggests an improvement or renewal of the whole. From the perspective of the "polis," self-fulfillment is less important than the survival of the race and the collective experience. What comedy does best is to bring the creaturely parts of the individual—biological, appetitive, isolated, or obsessive—into a communal form. Certainly we appreciate the individuality in Viola or Barbara Undershaft, Horner or Henry Carr, but all these characters are fully formed at the beginning and we need primarily to see how "it" will turn out. This "it" in comedy encompasses both the impersonal, performatory elements of delight that display the dexterity of the plotting as well as the collective, ethical order that is social, impersonal, and objective. We want to see characters consumed, so to speak, in the social occasion in which we participate. A character like Falstaff resides on the borderline of comedy because no social occasion can fully contain him, at least, perhaps, until *The Merry Wives of Windsor*. Touchstone as a wit disappears into his marriage in *As You Like It*. Just so, Jaques must leave that comic world; he comes from tragedy not because he is melancholy but because he is ethically individuated. And because Malvolio is individuated by his anger, he cannot be absorbed into the social occasion of the multiple marriages and must be entreated to peace somewhere offstage. When we ask "tragic" questions of comic characters, we often find that our sense of character abrades our sense of event. The very impersonality of comic

3. Wesley Trimpi, *Muses of One Mind: The Literary Analysis of Experience and Its Continuity* (Princeton, N.J.: Princeton University Press, 1983), p. 302. "The historical or legendary anonymity of the characters [in comedy] permits them often to become recognizable general types whose interrelationships must be restipulated by the action of each new exercise or play. The particular delightfulness of the plot arises from its plausible resolution of the initially enigmatic stipulations of the given situation. Since the persons, being more typical than individually 'known,' are to be characterized primarily through incident, the given circumstances must be clearly 'propounded' if the author's ingenuity is to appear in their analysis and synthesis. He must satisfy our need for logical arrangement by a 'dialectic' of character and incident rather than by arousing emotions strong enough to make us acquiesce in a catastrophe."

teleology makes it possible to accept the pairing of Angelo and Mariana at the end of *Measure for Measure* in spite of possible characterological or ethical problems; and it explains why Vivie Warren poses such a difficulty in *Mrs. Warren's Profession* when she rejects marriage in favor of work. Her choice of work goes against the grain of collective happiness in favor of individual self-determination. The "it" of comedy constitutes, finally, the consumption of the individual by the collective social world.

Marriage is just such an impersonal social form, absorbing personal character into social ritual and giving shape, at the same time, to any action that has preceded it. In the delight of performance that is unformed by the "duration" of narrative development, the only conclusion is cessation. Fatigue offers the only "reason" to stop. We often find, for example, that plays in the performatory mode have difficulties in ending. The plot is serial rather than causal. Volpone and Mosca cease their activities because they are "cut off" by the law. A Stoppard comedy can be exhausting because every moment is comic and the narrative line is tenuous. Marriage as a culmination to a comedy satisfies the narrative desire for form. It is especially appropriate for comedy, however, because it ritually signifies continuation. If continuation is the "desire" of the performatory mode because performance has no duration, marriage makes an ending even as it implies a beginning and a continuation. For as comedy leans toward the extreme of delight without endurance, we find a nostalgia for form. The temporal problem of comedy is exactly what Feste sings of at the end of *Twelfth Night*. Comedy is quotidian in structure rather than in subject matter alone. It imitates not "who" we are but "how" we are. The comedian must constantly repeat himself; he needs to reiterate and replay the pleasure of the comic performance because there is no duration in it. The comedy offers pleasures and delights that cannot stay, it must "strive to please you every day." And that is the pleasure Feste knows finally must be paid, either with emptiness or death.

The particular strategies for combining use and delight, collective durability and immediacy, have little to do with comic structure, however. That Viola, Olivia, Barbara Undershaft, Alithea, Indiana, Lucinda, and Cecily Cardew all marry at the conclusion of their respective comedies tells us something about a habit in comic structure but not necessarily anything about the signification of the marriages. Certainly part of our generic desire for the ingenues is to see them married, but we also want to see how skillfully the playwright can delay the marriage and how happily we can linger in performance. The specific marriage takes its significance from the qualities of that delay. Viola's marriage to Orsino, for example, has a different meaning from that of Barbara Undershaft's to Cusins or Alithea's to Harcourt. Henry Carr's marriage to Cecily is hardly identical to that of Bevil and Indiana. What I have previously called the rhetorical force of a comedy identifies how a particular playwright locates his use and delight, his durable forms and his performance techniques.

In Shaw, for example, we delight in the musicality of language and in the sleight of hand that makes ideas seem to appear. There is pleasure, furthermore, in the surprise of his paradoxes. What endures for Shaw is the form of paradox, which he uses to correct perception and reason. The work of his plays is to reform our perceptions and to show us paradox and contradiction under every conventional social rock. But as every assertion conceals its opposite, so Shaw's utilitarian and dystopian vision of men "as they are" conceals a deeper utopian ideal of a world that is as clean, efficient, and rational as Perivale St. Andrews. The sentimental comedy, on the other hand, is utilitarian and utopian. It seeks to mythologize persons of tender sentiment and to create an image of society based upon such people. It conceals, however, the dystopia of an economic system in which the downtrodden and oppressed are essential to the demonstration of goodness. The rhetoric of the sentimental comedy is "aphoristic" in that its value structure asserts an absolute certainty about its moral premises; it functions as the example of the social and moral precepts that determine the action of the plays. Like the Restoration comedy, the sentimental comedy presents a closed world; but instead of enclosing a single social stratum, the

sentimental comedy encompasses a scheme of personal, social, and divine order. Ethical action gains the sanction of divine imperative in speech and character as well as in the
premise. Sentimental comedy, in the terms I have been developing,
is all duration and form. It eliminates as much as possible the
transient elements of performance to focus on the interior and
enduring elements of human emotion and ethical choice. The
desire for durability and the aesthetic choices of character and
action that lead the audience toward "permanent" value and
character constitute the usefulness of the sentimental comedy.
Inasmuch as we respond to the interior "warmth" of character
and action, we may also find delight in such use, to be sure.
And in less overtly sentimental comedies, such as those of
Farquhar or Goldsmith, we do delight in character. By contrast, however, the "form" of Restoration comedy is wholly
formal. All exteriority and spectacle, it delights in the performance of its own wit, so that its usefulness, if any, disintegrates in the moment.

Comic rhetoric combines elements of sympathy and judgment, persuasion and passion by which we apprehend value,
character, and norm. It represents the combination of use and
delight. Because the combination is bound in language, it is
also bound in history and changing social values and perceptions. Comedies from cultures and languages other than the
British comedies I discuss here might well draw a different
map between the poles of *utile* and *dulce*, utopia and dystopia.
The polarities are constant, but the strategies and gravita-
tional forces, if you will, can change the territory.

For a brief illustration, we can look at Molière and locate the
tensions of use and delight, utopian and dystopian values,
but we will need to name another "rhetorical axis." Molière
centers his plays on humored characters, dystopian centers
who are the source of our delight as they display their obsessions, hypocrisies, or pretensions. These dystopian characters, however, are surrounded by a society of normal or reasonable characters, who usually want no more than the right
marriage and an orderly life. The norm of the *raisonneur* bal-

ances the dystopian characters. A clear-minded Cleante, for example, establishes a utopian idea of the rational life: his reasonable sense and humanity counter the absurdity of Orgon and the hypocrisy of Tartuffe. Molière's dystopia is surrounded by a utopia. The obsessive characters of Molière are, like Jonson's, analytics of particular moral diseases. They are placed, however, in the context of a set of unifying or synthesizing characters who create the larger world of goodwill, reason, tolerance, and understanding. Orgon may be seduced temporarily by the appeal of Tartuffe, but he is finally integrated into the utopia of his family, which is further integrated into the larger utopia of the king's all-knowing rule. The mixture is unlike the Jonsonian dystopia in which all characters are obsessed and create the totality of Jonson's horizon. Any sense of utopia in Jonson, of what "ought" to be, is displaced beyond the realm of the play. Molière brings his utopia into the structure of the play.

The accuracy and precision of Molière's language, like that of his characters, delights us primarily by display. We do not ask for depth of motive or range of feeling: we find subtlety and nuance in the reductive form of the couplet that brings clarity, logic, balance, and reason to language. We might thus put Molière on an axis called balance, with the defining characteristic of *raison*. The world of the play may reflect a particular society, but it is largely a mental world, conceived and executed with the formal values of logic, clarity, balance, and reason. The couplet form creates an aesthetic balance between reason and passion, a volatile mixture contained only by form. Likewise, the various displays of the dystopian characters threaten to explode into real danger but are contained by the surrounding society. The reduction of both character and language to the gracefulness of the couplet form creates a display that has moral signification without any duration. The dystopian characters gather our disapproval, but we also delight in their displays. We further delight in the restoration of order and balance. But that final restoration is less a matter of actual justice than of formal symmetry. Implications of both moral and social meaning are present, but the initial pleasure is found in the elegance of the formal balance. The moral components of characters are merely masks of utility. The greater value seems to lie in elegant order and symmetry, for which the moral features of characters are an opportunity. The moral order in Molière, in other words, conceals a "deeper" interest in the delights of performance. It is more significant that at the end of *Tartuffe* a formal order comes to rest than that the young Mariane must no longer marry Tartuffe.

One way of attaching meaning to a comic ending is to examine the qualities of rhetoric and intention. In *Tartuffe*, Mariane's marital status becomes almost incidental. The marriage of Bevil and Indiana, however, constitutes the proof that persistent selflessness along with dutiful behavior is a self-fulfilling good. It encloses human affairs in the divine enclosure of Providence. Conversely, the marriage of Barbara and Cusins signifies the acceptance of the paradox that "the way of life is through the factory of death." They join the social utopia founded on that paradox. The reported marriage of Henry Carr and Cecily in *Travesties* is Stoppard's version of the paradoxical marriage of the fictional and the historical that constitutes the methodology of that play. And the marriage of Alithea and Harcourt suggests that wit is the way to win a bride, for through witty deception Harcourt shows Alithea her misplaced loyalties.

In the exchanges between use and delight, rhetoric becomes the means of persuasion to a value. For example, part of our difficulty with Restoration comedies comes from their deeply ambivalent position in the realms of pure artificiality and dystopian vision. The Restoration comedy of manners does reflect an "actual" society and the manners and mores of a particular stratum, but they are such manners that we cannot ethically admire them. Our admiration, rather, is aesthetic if we admire them at all. We temporarily change our ethical attitudes (for example, the attitude that cuckolding is wrong) to suit the aesthetic force and consequently give wit and success the highest value on our ethical scale. Wycherley gives a nod to an ethical norm in Alithea, but the center of our delighted interest is Horner. Indeed, the aesthetic commitment to Horner creates an almost perfect equilibrium between the dystopian vision (what is wrong with this world) and an ideal (but how perfectly it is wrong). In *The Country Wife* there is an almost total moral inversion—so complete that we are willing to suspend our ethical beliefs, join in the celebration of wit, and wonder at its amoral perfection. Wit is the language of complete assurance in one's moral or social position. Here, moral inversion is asserted with the determination of truth. The Restoration assertiveness teaches us how the aesthetic appeal of comedy can actually convert our own ethical structures. What in reality might be the worst of worlds can be in art the most delightful. Assertiveness itself in the tone of the aphorism is a source of delight, converting even ethically negative behavior into comic virtue.

The wit of the Restoration, however, can conceal an implicit sentimental value. We may delight in the wit and success of Horner, for example, but we feel morally "safe" in the honesty and truehearted love of Alithea and Harcourt. Although they are unlike the "conscious" lovers of sentimental comedies, their true feeling presents a sentimental value. Feeling, in other words, is the antidote for wit. The "honest" love between Alithea and Harcourt allows us to enjoy the unfeeling, dishonest wit of Horner all the more. I do not mean to suggest that sentimentality is the deeper content of the Restoration comedy. But sentimentality is the specific remedy for Restoration sensibility, directly opposed to its attitudes, perspectives, qualities, and intents. If the Restoration dystopia is all surface and form, the sentimental world is all depth and sincerity. If the Restoration dystopia asserts the aesthetic artifice of wit and successful gamesmanship, the sentimental utopia asserts the moral example of benevolence, sincerity, generosity, and high-mindedness.

The rhetorical axes define differences and similarities among comedies that appear only to differ. The spectrum from use to delight, utopia to dystopia further suggests similarities in unlikely pairs such as Stoppard and Wycherley or Shaw and Steele. Wycherley joins Stoppard at the *dulce* end of the spectrum because his artifice is the primary source of our delight. Both playwrights enjoy the action of pure play, one in the mind, the other in society. They diverge in that Stoppard integrates paradoxical elements in a synthesis of logical impossibilities and artifice. Wycherley's anatomy of Restoration society is diagnostic and analytic, though not finally judgmental. Likewise, sentimental comedy joins Shaw at the high end of the spectrum of *utile*. Shaw might well complain that his comedies respond to the moral certainties of bourgeois sentimentalists, and Shaw's paradoxical style is clearly distinct from the aphoristic style of moral certainties. Both his plays and the sentimental comedies, however, are concerned about social and political morality, not about pure artifice or art for its own sake. Although their attitudes and styles differ, they are in the same realm of usefulness.

In any particular case, a comedy draws from any or all attitudes and intentions. The diagram in chapter 1 (p. 12) maps relative values and strategies; it offers a way of seeing relations between many different comedies as well as tensions in a single comedy. It also suggests that comedy does have a history. One can see historical forces at work in the development of comic projects, for example, as *poesis* changes to aphorism and to paradox. At the same time, however, these elements are not bound to a single historical period. I am not presently concerned with either historical causes or the reasons that comic methodology responds to changing cultural climate. The map implies, however, that the history of comedy parallels that of tragedy. The tragic realism of Ibsen, for example, could be seen as an extension of Shaw's dystopian *utile*, melodrama as the unhappy version of the utopian *utile* of sentimentality. The positive nihilism of Beckett is the tragic extension of Stoppard in the territory of utopian *dulce*; and Jacobean tragedy, with its spectacular gore, is a version of Wycherley's territory of dystopian *dulce*. Shakespeare and Jonson diverge in utopian and dystopian attitudes in their metaphysical and historical tragedies, but they would still be at the midpoint between *utile* and *dulce*. I am not planning to press these connections beyond this suggestion, but I do not want to ignore the ethical thread that binds both comedies and tragedies and is wound stylistically to historical change; for comedy, like tragedy, does have an ethical history.

Comedy is an acute instance of the problem of fiction. Fictional forms both present and represent; they can imitate a society and accommodate ethical structures; literary and theatrical forms can both transfix us and teach us, delight and instruct. Comedy is an acute form because it seems to favor delight over instruction, but it is so ethically involved that it cannot avoid didacticism. It emphasizes the "danger" of representation: that the imitation itself creates a model. The strict moralist fears that comedy will reflect the worst in human society and that the reflection will become an imitated object. Such a moralist is not necessarily wrong. Shaw, for one, believed that the harmless laughter of comedy could move people to accept a new or socially dangerous idea. A comedy can add to a repository of possibilities and open up the boundaries of conventional restrictions. The rupture of the ethical and social boundary may at first be invisible or recognized only as an absurdity, but laughter at an absurdity stretches the boundary of possibilities. New images and ideas gradually integrate with a whole functional system. The moral critic is fearful that we will digest comedy's "deformities" because, coated with delight, they go down so easily. Yet it is the task of the comic playwright to manipulate ethical ambiguities and to locate comic rupture in the anxiety between "oughts" and "wants." With one attitude comedy sees the failures of the world, morally, ethically, socially; it ridicules, condemns, corrects, uproots, and subverts. With the opposite attitude it sympathizes, celebrates, accepts, confirms, and embraces. The comic attitude is a restless one: it disrupts the norm even as it creates one; it disturbs our values even as it delights.

Index

Compositor: Wilsted & Taylor
Text: 10/12 Palatino
Display: Palatino
Printer: Braun-Brumfield, Inc.
Binder: Braun-Brumfield, Inc.